Consider Islam
Disproving the Patriots of Propaganda

Kenny Bomer

ISBN: 9781095189351

Library of Congress Control Number

Islamic emblems created by Linda "iLham" Barto, copyright 2006

Printed in the United States of America.

Published by:

For reprint permission or other communication, contact the author:
Kenny Bomer
2701 Helena Street #402
Houston, TX 77006
mujahid.kbomer@gmail.com

Author's note: I express my deep and sincere appreciation to the publisher for seeing the value of this work and making it come to fruition351

About the Author

Kenny Bomer (Mujahid Islam) is a thirty-year revert to Islam from Christianity. He currently resides in Houston, Texas, and is the president of the Brazosport Islamic Society in Lake Jackson, Texas, located an hour south of Houston. He is a student of Mishkah University where he is pursuing a bachelor's degree in Islamic Studies. He is an independent  researcher in the field of comparative religions, a public speaker and debater, and a community activist having organized numerous food/blanket drives to feed the homeless and needy in both Houston and Lake Jackson. Kenny Bomer is a former hip-hop artist having signed two record deals in his life with the record labels Mr. Henry/Ichiban Records (1986) and King B Music (2000). He became a certified Protection and Response (PAR) instructor with the Department of Juvenile Justice through Cypress Creek Juvenile Corrections facility in Crystal River, Florida, where he was qualified to train employees in crisis intervention and self-defense/take-down tactics and is currently a certified API (510) Pressure Vessel Inspector through the American Petroleum Institute.

At the age of eleven, he became a ward of the state after he and his younger brother were abandoned shortly after his parents separated. He became a resident of the Brazoria County Youth Home (BCYH) in Freeport, Texas, where he lived until the age of eighteen. While residing at the BCYH, he was first exposed to religion through Christian employees of the BCYH who attended Assemblies of God Churches. It was during that time that he was also exposed to Islam through his partner in music who became a member of the Nation of Islam, best known by Malcom X, Louis Farrakhan, and Elijah Muhammad. He embraced Orthodox Islam at the age of seventeen after reading the Qur'an for the first time, and through examining the religion of Islam during his own independent studies and research.

Table of Contents

Dedicated to my sons

Benjermen Scott Bomer

and

Ruben James Bomer

Introduction

Without Islam, I am incapable of maneuvering through this world and all the obstacles that it presents. I can't do it. I have tried. I have failed. The continuous return to prayer five times each day, and the continuous consciousness and remembrance of, Allah (blessed and exalted is He), has been vital in my ability to cope with some very difficult events that have transpired in my life. No, I have not always lived in the obedience of Allah (Arabic for *God*), but in His wisdom, He has called me back to Himself through the mercy of a series of tests and trials that have caused me to look at life with a whole new understanding.

One of those tests came in the form of an event that I would have to describe as my worst nightmare come true. Now as I look back on it, I realize that what I once seen as my greatest nightmare was actually my greatest blessing! That experience provided me with new perspective regarding my need to rely upon Allah more than anyone or anything in this world. That experience made me feel as though I was dying over and over again while living through it, but it was that same experience that gave me new life. All praise is due to Allah.

I intend to write another book about that event in the near future, *Insha Allah* (God willing), and so I will not go into specifics in this book regarding that past event, but I want to express to the reader that hardships and difficulties in life are a mercy from Allah which are meant to draw your attention to Him. Sometimes those things are going to be so overwhelming that you think you will never rebound from it. Some people will turn to things of this world for comfort, some will lash out, some will wish for death, and some will even kill themselves because they feel that there is no escape, but there is always an escape for those who turn to Allah sincerely.

"Be sure We shall test you with something of fear and hunger, some loss in goods, lives and the fruits [of your toil], but give glad tidings to those who patiently persevere —who say, when afflicted with calamity, 'From Allah we come, and to Him is our return.' They are those on whom [descend] blessings from their Lord and mercy, and they are the ones who receive guidance."

Surah Al-Baqarah 2: 155-157

This book is a way to give back, and it is a means of thanking and bringing praise to Allah (blessed and exalted is He) for helping me to endure as patiently as possible the difficulties with which I have been faced. Writing this book is a form of worship, and the fact that I have taken on such a task is proof of how Allah (blessed and exalted is He) will take you to a better place, even if it means traveling a difficult and chaotic path to get there. Everything is a test. Islam is the answer.

My intention for this book is to defend Islam against falsehood and misconceptions that have been used to tarnish this way of life, which is a true source of peace and comfort for those who humble themselves in sincere submission to our Creator. It is not my intention to offend any individual or group with anything that I say. My objective is to present information to the reader that will cause them to realize that what has been presented to them about Islam may or may not be true, as antagonists fervently and routinely make false and erroneous claims. I am simply asking the reader to consider what is presented fairly, in order to decipher for one's self what Islam is, while rejecting what it is not. Writing this book may be the most important thing I ever do in my life. May Allah accept my efforts. Ameen.

1

Normalizing Hatred & Bigotry

As a student of comparative religions, I have studied both Islam and Christianity extensively, and, though I don't claim to be a scholar or historian, I pray that with the help of Allah (blessed and exalted is He), I can convey the truth about both religions. It is also my intention to address the slanderous claims of atheists and known Islamophobes, from a reasonable and logical perspective, while distinguishing false and erroneous information from that which is factual, regarding the truth and beauty of Islam.

By doing so, I will demonstrate why Islam is the fastest growing religion in every country throughout the world. The Pew Research Center says, "Islam will nearly equal Christianity in its number of followers by 2050 before eclipsing it around 2070, if current trends continue." On average, there have been 30,000 new converts to Islam each year in the United States, most of whom are Women, since the infamous 9/11 attacks carried out by those that have been wrongly labeled as Muslims. This rise in followers can be associated with the fact that, before the 9/11 attacks, most people had very little knowledge of Islam and seldom heard the word mentioned. But the impact of 9/11 has caused a curiosity to arise in people for various reasons, with one of those being the fallacious desire to understand why and how a religion could cause people to commit murder in the name of that religion.

Those that can set aside their fears and prejudices in order to be earnest seekers of the truth have and will continue to come to the realization that there is nothing in Islam that promotes or even remotely suggests such actions as terrorism or any other type of oppression. The ability to see through the smokescreen of the never-relenting campaign of fear is crucial. One must be capable of understanding that propaganda and the dissemination of false information has, and always will be, utilized to sway the masses. This is done in order to achieve the desired goals of those in power that seem to be determined to normalize bigotry and hatred, as xenophobia combines with islamophobia, causing division amongst various groups in society.

The common man and woman most often have no choice other than to accept what has been told to them by those in power, who attempt to present themselves as trustworthy. But all one needs to do is consider the rhetoric of a man such as Donald J. Trump, and his inconsistencies regarding any given topic, in order to realize that we can't always trust those in power. We sometimes lose trust in close friends and family, so why should anyone assume that they can trust people that they don't know intimately? Yet many believe they can.

Some hear the phrase "radical Islam" and see images while hearing claims in the media of supposed members of ISIS, Al Qaeda, or the Taliban committing acts of terrorism. They are gradually brainwashed into thinking that Islam is the root cause of those atrocities. But the reality is, that out of the estimated 1.6 to 1.8 billion Muslims in the world today, a mere 0.00625% (less than 1%) have any affiliation with terrorism, based on studies conducted by the Pew Research Center. Yet we hear about that less-than-1% 99% of the time. That percentage amounts to approximately 15,000 people out of 1.6 to 1.8 billion Muslims. Despite that, people are persuaded to believe that they are at risk of being victimized by "radical Islamic terrorism", but there is no such thing because Islam has nothing to do with "radical terrorism". I will address this reality in upcoming chapters.

A study done in 2016 revealed that there are approximately 3.3 million Muslims living in the United States, which is about 1% of the total U.S. population. Yet some people are so naïve and gullible that they accept the belief that such a small minority is out to wreak havoc while trying to take over America, along with the rest of the world, while implementing Sharia Law. If you are one of those people, I must ask you, Have you seen anyone attempting such a task? Do you even know what Sharia Law is? Are you sure? Do you realize that most Muslims don't even know what Sharia Law is?

A study carried out by the University of North Carolina revealed that less than 0.0002% of Americans killed since 9/11 were killed by Muslims. We must realize that the American government must be aware of these statistics. So why is Islam continuously being discussed as though guilty, when the facts demonstrate the exact opposite? Another fact is that terrorists kill more Muslims than any other group of people in the world!

I encourage the reader to consider the fact that you are around Muslims almost daily while not even realizing it. Muslims are your doctors, law enforcement officers, military personnel, fire fighters, teachers, business owners, etc. We are in your local grocery stores and malls. We are your neighbors. We are made up of every nationality on Earth. Muslims, like you, are regular everyday people just trying to live a happy life in a world full of tests and trials. Muslims feel the same emotions and experience the same ups and downs that you do.

According to the *Huffington Post*, five out of the past twelve Nobel Peace Prize winners (42%) have been Muslims. This type of statistic doesn't garner much attention because it doesn't fit the slanderous labels or the agenda of those looking to discredit Islam from being, not "A", but "THE Religion of Peace". Muslim communities have lower crime rates, divorce rates, alcoholism rates, drug addiction rates, and fewer broken families than that of Christianity by far. Although Islam is 2nd behind Christianity in the overall number of followers, it is 1st in the number of "practicing followers". Let me explain why.

If you were to go into any mall, sporting event, or night club in the United States and ask random people what their religion is, 9 out of 10 would most likely say, "Christianity", while loading their shopping carts with alcohol and pork, buying $8.00 beers from the man walking up and down the steps of the stadium shouting, "Beer here! Get your ice-cold beer here!", and dressed in revealing outfits while drunk and twerking in the club. This example may sound a bit harsh, but it is true.

My intent is not to point a hypocritical finger at Christians, or to insinuate that there aren't Muslims who do these things as well, because there are. What I am trying to do is point out that, based on tradition and demographics, most people in the United States are going to claim that they are members of one of the 33,000 denominations of Christianity that exist in the world, yet they don't adhere to the teachings of Jesus (peace and blessings be upon him), and in most cases seldom attend church. Yes, you read right: 33, 000 distinct denominations!

Then there are those that might attend church every now and then or on holidays, while claiming to be followers of Christ. But didn't Jesus (peace and blessings be upon him) reportedly say in the Bible: (*Note: Christian Scholars of the Jesus Seminar reject the longer sayings of Jesus for being fabrications.*)

"Ye shall know them by their fruits. Do men gather grapes of thorns, or figs of thistles? Even so every good tree brings forth good fruit; but a corrupt tree brings forth evil fruit."? Matthew 7:16-17 (KJV)

Statistics prove that Islam is a far more disciplined and obedient way of life. But it certainly doesn't appear that way due to the constant assault that it endures, not only in the American media, but throughout the world. Yet if you compare the fruits of Islam and Christianity, throughout the history of man, by studying the historical and theological facts, you must conclude that something has been grossly twisted around and distorted. But doing so requires time and effort, to which most people have no interest in committing. It requires the ability to look at the big picture and to consider various occasions throughout history that have been passively viewed as atrocities, such as the case with the Christian Crusades, the slaughter and genocide of Native Americans, four hundred years of slavery, the bombing of

Hiroshima and Nagasaki, the 1st and 2nd Gulf War, and the War in Afghanistan, among other atrocities. Instead, these events are justified for one reason or another or swept under the rug by the United States, which is predominantly Christian.

Are those mass killings any less horrific than Adolph Hitler killing 6,000,000 Jews during the Holocaust, while claiming to be Christian? Christianity is guilty of far more killing than that of Islam throughout history; yet, Islam is demonized, and islamophobia runs rampant in our society, which is backed by the rhetoric of an obviously prejudiced and bigoted man such as Donald J. Trump. His hate-filled words have once again fueled and stimulated the deep-rooted prejudices that are hidden in the shadows of American society. First it was the Native Americans that were targeted, then African Americans, Japanese citizens, and now Muslims and anyone of color, such as the immigrants seeking to come to the United States to better the circumstances and futures of their families, like the influx of Europeans which began in 1492. Each of the afore mentioned groups are either past or current targets of a "Christian America", that is sheltered behind its hidden agendas and mass propaganda campaigns that have seemed to routinely normalize hatred and bigotry throughout history.

Many people (usually Caucasian) become very angry at the mention of those periods of American history, as if they are being thrown under the bus and being held responsible for the actions of their ancestors. But my objective, as a White American Muslim, is to use those dreadful periods as examples of how history repeats itself. Those crimes against humanity were well planned and executed campaigns by those who held positions of power, and we see some of their tactics, slogans, and rhetoric being utilized in current times. Accomplishing such campaigns require the help of commoners, both then and now, who are or have been manipulated into thinking that they are uniting under a just cause. Such campaigns are meant to stimulate solidarity and unity in the country, giving people a common goal to achieve as they unite under the same cause, even if it is unjust.

It is obvious that an overwhelming number of people in the United States, as well as throughout the world, are in fear of the unknown, and so they are eager to build up walls of divisiveness instead of building bridges granting access to equality, dignity, and human rights for all. The people in power are more stricken with fear than anyone, as they fight to keep their status by turning neighbor against neighbor, race against race, nation against nation, and religion against religion. Islam is the answer for it all. I will demonstrate throughout the course of this book that Islam guides people to just and fair treatment for all of mankind regardless of race, nationality, or economic status. Islam directs people to feed the hungry and shelter the homeless and to fight against all forms of oppression and injustice. Islam draws our attention to our Creator and the instincts that He has instilled within everyone as to what is right and wrong. It is our obligation as brothers and sisters in humanity to follow that guidance.

During his last sermon, Prophet Muhammad (peace and blessings be upon him) made the following statement:

"All mankind is from Adam and Eve. An Arab has no superiority over a non-Arab, and a non-Arab has no superiority over an Arab; also a white has no superiority over a black, and a black has no superiority over a white, except by piety and good action."

This sermon was delivered on the ninth day of Dhul al Hijjah 10 A.H (632 A.C.). in the 'Uranah valley of Mount Arafat.

Islam dismantles and tears down walls that hatred and bigotry erect. Some of the walls are literal structures comprised of concrete and steel, but the walls that play on the thoughts, beliefs, and emotions of the masses are the walls that truly separate people. Those walls of hatred and bigotry are tools of divisiveness that erect barriers among groups who hold various beliefs and ideologies, which are commonly centered around the economic status of each. So it is of no surprise that a man such as Donald Trump, who has lived a life of luxury, would fight so aggressively to erect a barrier or wall to keep out "those [brown] people over there" as if they are subhuman or animalistic in nature.

Hatred and bigotry have been utilized in various campaigns as people of color have been vilified and dehumanized by people of the so-called "upper crust" of society who have all too often used religion as a justification for their wrong doing. This is evident by the "Mark of Cain" verses of the Bible which have led many people throughout history to believe that all black people are cursed because they are descendants of Cain, who they say was blackened by God because he killed his brother Abel. Another example for the justification of hatred and bigotry are the "Curse of Ham" verses in the Bible. There are many others as well.

The most obvious example of how Christianity has influenced people towards racism are the paintings and sculptures of what has been presented as Jesus the son of Mary (peace and blessings be upon them), depicting them as being Caucasians with European features, despite the Bible describing Jesus (peace and blessings upon him) as having feet the color of burnt brass with hair like lamb's wool, as referenced in the Bible.

This has a subliminal effect on both whites and non-whites alike as the Christian perception of God has been presented to the world as a white man. This gives whites a sense of entitlement while incorporating verses describing man as being made in God's image in the Bible, whom they believe is white, causing some to subconsciously or even openly express their "better than thou" attitudes in various ways while dealing with people of other races and nationalities. Non-whites are also affected subliminally as they pray to a "white god" while hanging up paintings of a so-called white Jesus (peace and blessings be upon him) in their homes and churches, while wearing crosses bearing similar images around their necks. This causes them to inherently feel as though they are somehow less in stature than

17

whites as they submit and accept many subliminal as well as openly blatant messages which promote white superiority and privilege. Addressing this issue would require me to write another book in order to address this issue thoroughly and adequately, but the signs are there in plain sight for anyone willing to take an honest look.

These issues are seldom discussed openly and honestly among some people, because it is easier to simply ignore them, and that is the case for whites and non-whites alike. I mention this because of the obvious hypocrisy in it all, as hatred, bigotry, racism, fear, and prejudice all combine as a hidden and deep-rooted vice that squeezes the heart of society, pitting brothers of humanity against one another. This is a disgusting and painful reality as some people are absorbed in or affected by prejudice more or less than others, causing them to either be more subtle or aggressive in attitudes and behaviors while dealing with people of other nations and/or races.

Despite which role one plays, either the oppressors or the oppressed, or those who speak out against oppression, we each have a responsibility. Some operate covertly or subtly, while some speak out aggressively. The subtle approach is no less harmful than the aggressive as both have a detrimental effect in a one two punch either for or against society. We have seen this occurring in current times with the Muslim ban in 2016, which I adamantly stood protesting against at the George W. Bush Intercontinental Airport here in Houston, TX. It is also seen in the bigoted fight by those seeking to keep immigrants out of the country by erecting a wall at the Texas/Mexico border. This is like shunning and spitting in the faces of our Mexican neighbors who are simply wanting to make a better life for themselves in the great melting pot that we call the United States of America.

But what happens when some of the ingredients that make up that pot are tainted, soured, spoiled, or simply won't dissolve into the mix, as is the case with those who prefer to segregate themselves from those that may look, talk, think, or believe differently than they do? This type of mentality produces a poisoned concoction that is unhealthy for all members of society as people play a systematic game of "follow the leader" despite whether the leader is for or against the individual or group. The people being oppressed often play along with the charade because it is easier than standing up against oppression. Those who refuse to speak up to dissolve the issues are guilty of sitting idle as injustices occur. Those who are prone to follow the oppressor as endorsers of the injustices are obviously guilty of backing the atrocities against others. Despite one's role, the responsibility lies on all who allow oppression of any kind to take place.

We have seen signs of this occur in a much larger and more atrocious scale in modern times as the Palestinians have been slaughtered by the millions and their country destroyed by Israel as the world just sits by watching in amusement, with the United States sitting front and center as Muslims have war crimes enacted against them. The genocide of the Palestinian people has been taking place for years; yet, no one in our local or foreign governments has spoken out against Israel because of the economic and, ironically, religious ties that the United States has with Israel in its powerful influence on the world. The irony is that the "Christian" United States routinely fights to defend Israel while Jewish people reject Jesus (peace and blessings be upon him) while the Palestinian Muslims believe in him. An article of faith in Islam states that one simply is not a Muslim if he or she does not believe in Jesus (peace and blessings be upon him) as a prophet and the Messiah.

I am by no means suggesting that the United States or any other country should stand for or against Israel based on religion. As a Muslim, I do not believe in oppression of people for any reason. I am simply pointing out the willingness of others to accept the crimes of humanity committed against the Palestinian people. Be it for economic ties to Israel or because the "Christians" believe that all of this will trigger the return of Jesus (peace and blessings be upon him), who they believe will rule the earth from Israel. The silence of people of power

19

Kenny Bomer

and prestige is cacophonous, as they have cowardly refused to speak out against those atrocities.

That is until one of the first two Muslim women elected to congress, Rep. Ilhan Omar, spoke out against Israel on Twitter saying, *"It's all about the Benjamins baby."* Her implication was that support for Israel was bought. Journalist Glenn Greenwald tweeted an article about how Minority Leader Kevin McCarthy (R-CA) wanted to punish Omar and Rep. Rashida Tlaib (D-MI) over their so-called anti-Semitic rhetoric. Both Omar and Tlaid are people of color and are Semitic themselves, relating to the peoples who speak Semitic languages, especially Aramaic, Hebrew, and Arabic.

It is of no surprise to me that it was Muslim women who spoke in defense of the Palestinian people only weeks after their being elected into the United States Congress. Women are generally, more emotional and compassionate, and that often generates a strength and courage that men may lack when dealing with certain issues. Women are by nature far better nurturers than men, and they are more prone to run to the rescue of those in need. It is Islam and the instincts given to us by our Creator that persuade Muslims to speak out against oppression and injustice, but those stories aren't as news worthy as they go against the grain of the campaigns used to slander Islam, Muslims, and the best of examples on how to treat people in society, Prophet Muhammad (peace and blessings be upon him). Note what Allah says in the following chapter of the Qur'an:

"O you who believe, stand out firmly for justice, as witnesses to Allah, even as against yourselves, or your parents or your kin, and whether it be (against) rich or poor."

Surah An-Nisa 4: 135

Just as equally, it is of no surprise that those courageous female ambassadors of the truth and beauty of Islam would immediately be put under the radar and targeted by the President of the United States

20

himself, who stated the following in responding to an apology issued by Rep. Omar, during a live press conference:

"I think she should either resign from Congress, or she should certainly resign from the house foreign affairs committee. What she said is so deep seeded in her heart that her lame apology.... that's what it was, it was lame....and she didn't mean a word of it...uh, it was just not appropriate. I think she should resign from Congress."

His choice of words was strategic by implying that something "deep seeded" in her heart is what led her to speak out. Of course, his attempt was to make a slanderous implication about Islam. Yet I agree that it was indeed Islam that led her to speak out in truth about a well-known but hushed and shadowy fact about the secret agendas of those in power. That comment came from a man who twice equated the white supremacists in Charlottesville, NC., to the protestors speaking out against them. These were white supremacists chanting, "Blood and Soil", a Nazi phrase for racial purity.

Islam is the answer for all these issues as well as every issue that mankind will ever face during the course of our lives. But there must be a willingness in the hearts of people to seek the truth and to be just, while standing against all forms of oppression despite one's race, nationality, gender, or religion. It is a truth that benefits all of those who choose to follow a straight path of righteousness and decency, and it is for these reasons that I implore the reader to open your heart and mind, and to consider Islam. But I am only obligated as a Muslim to tell you about Islam; it is up to you to choose to receive it.

"Let there be no coercion in religion. Truth stands out clear from error. Whoever rejects evil and believes in Allah has grasped the most trustworthy handhold that never breaks. And Allah hears and knows all things."

Surah Al-Baqarah 2: 256

2
Just the Basics

Islam has indeed been a trustworthy handhold for me, as well as approximately 1.8 Billion Muslims worldwide that have experienced true Islam. I am deeply saddened and dismayed when I hear someone making derogatory comments about Islam in person or in the media, without knowing the beauty that is securely harnessed within it.

Some people hear or see the word *Islam*, and then instantaneously put up barriers within their minds due to misconceptions and misleading information obtained through illegitimate sources such as social media, news, television, and the movie industry, which villainize Islam and its followers. Islam by definition means, "submission to the will of God". So why would anyone attempt to villainize those that submit to our Creator? I am referring to the God of all creation who sent the prophets Adam, Noah, Moses, Abraham, Jesus, and His final Messenger, Prophet Muhammad, as well as many others, to give guidance to mankind (peace and blessings upon them all).

We as Muslims worship no one and no thing, other than our Creator. The definition for the word *Muslim* is, "one who submits to the will of God". It certainly does not mean "terrorist", contrary to popular belief. Throughout this book, I will be using the English word *God* and the Arabic word *Allah* in various places, while referring to our Creator, so that non-Muslims can get better acquainted with associating the word *Allah* with being the Creator. I will do this to help correct misconceptions held by those who are under the impression that Muslims worship some foreign God unfamiliar with non-Muslims. The Arabic word *Allah* is a unique word comprised of two separate Arabic words: *Al*, which means "the", and *iLah*, which means

"God". By combining these two words, we get the phrase *the God*, in the English language, or *Allah*, in Arabic. The use of the word *Allah*, in the Arabic language, is very important for Muslims because it distinguishes and places the Creator above all other so-called gods. Using the word *God*, makes it easier for some people to relate to what is being said, so I will use that word as well because it is a familiar term for them.

When talking to non-Muslims, I often use the Spanish word for *God*, which is *Dios*, as an example to draw attention to the use of synonymous words of various languages --to bring them to a better understanding. So plainly, the Arabic word for *God* is *Allah*, like the Spanish word for *God* is *Dios*, while we simply say *God* in English.

The lack of understanding regarding something that is so easy to comprehend is disturbing to me, because we live in an age where information can be easily accessed through the internet, although not all sources of information are accurate. But spending a little time and effort can lead you to the truth if you go about the process of verifying information by utilizing various respected sources. Yet some, with information right there at their fingertips waiting to be accessed, wrongly believe that Muslims worship someone other than our Creator because of the word *Allah*, yet they don't make that same false presumption about those who use the word *Dios* while referencing God in Spanish. That is because Islam has been strategically targeted and vilified, not only in the United States, but throughout the world.

In the English language, one may hear the word *God*, which could bring to mind a variety of different beings that have been given that title; such as, Zeus, Poseidon, Thor, numerous Greek or Hindu gods, and, yes, even Jesus (peace be upon him), as well as many others. But it is important for Muslims to let it be known that we worship the God who is the Creator of all, who is without partners or equals, and that we do not worship anyone else. So, all Muslims use the word *Allah*, regardless of what nationality one belongs.

Some people use the names Jehovah, Yahweh, Adonai, and

Elohim when referring to God. Jesus (peace be upon him) spoke Aramaic and used a word similar to *Allah*, which is *AaLaH*, according to an Aramaic dictionary. These names are common for some people, while they are highly uncommon for others. None of these are English names, yet people associate them with being God, even if they themselves never use them. So why is it that people seem to lose all sense of logic when they hear the name *Allah*? Some even associate the name with evil. They are mistaken. They simply aren't aware of the fact that the Bible, translated into Arabic, also uses the word *Allah*. That is because Arabic speakers from all religious backgrounds (Muslims, Christians, and Jews) use the word *Allah* to mean *God*. I must point out that less than 7% of the world's population of Muslims is Arab, and not all Arabs are Muslims! There are many Christian and Jewish Arabs, and they all use the word *Allah*.

It is ridiculous, aggravating, and sometimes comical, hearing people making comments suggesting that Muslims worship some alternate being or a "Black Box" in the desert, or a "Moon God", simply due to their lack of knowledge. They don't realize that the "Black Box" to which they refer is the Kaaba. This is a structure that many scholars believe was originally built by Prophet Adam (peace be upon him) and then re-built or repaired by Prophet Abraham and his son Ishmael (peace be upon them) as directed by Allah (blessed and exalted is He). Muslims believe that our Creator sent a black meteorite to earth to designate the place for the Kaaba to be built, and that the Kaaba sits directly below the throne of Allah. There are references to the Kaaba in Christianity which acknowledges the structure as "the house that Abraham built", referenced in the Bible.

"Unto the place of the altar, which he had made there at the first: and there Abram called on the name of the LORD."

Genesis 13: 4 (KJV)

Muslims do not worship the Kaaba, but we turn towards it in prayer like Prophet Abraham (peace be upon him) did and as directed by Allah (blessed and exalted is He) in the Holy Qur'an.

"We see the turning of your face [for guidance] to the heavens. Now We shall turn you to a direction that shall please you. Turn then your face in the direction of the Sacred Mosque; wherever you are, turn your faces in that direction. The People of the Book [Christians and Jews] know well that that is the truth from their Lord, and Allah is not unmindful of what they do."

Surah Al-Baqarah 2: 144

The word *Kaaba* is derived from the Arabic word *Qiblah*, which means the direction that should be faced when a Muslim is engaged in prayers. This is the same type of action that is practiced in Judaism. Jews outside of Israel pray in the direction of Israel; Jews in Israel pray in the direction of Jerusalem; Jews in Jerusalem pray in the direction of the Temple Mount; Jews on the Temple Mount pray in the direction of the Holy of Holies. No one knows exactly where the Holy of Holies stood, but it is known that the Foundation Stone was located within it. Today the Foundation Stone lies under the Dome of the Rock. But Jews aren't accused of worshipping the Dome of the Rock. So why are Muslims accused of worshipping the Kaaba?

The purpose of turning a certain direction in prayer represents togetherness and uniformity among followers. It is as if to say, "We are all in one accord", which is a common saying in Christianity, even though Christians do not turn towards any particular direction while praying. There are those who are uncomfortable with anything that is unfamiliar to them, so they are quick to label something or someone that is outside of their comfort zone, with some derogatory name or connotation. This is the case with many people even despite varying levels of intellect. If something does not fall within their comfort zone, they see it as foreign, and so they often become defensive in order to guard and protect their own beliefs, understandings, or opinions.

without even realizing it. So instead of opening themselves up to learning something new, they are prejudiced and judgmental. They are often quick to shun others, or they will strike out against those with different understandings, opinions, or beliefs.

If you are open to learning about other beliefs, then you must consider the sources for the information to which you are exposed, because our society is routinely saturated with false and deceptive information. Such information is usually uneducated rumors and hearsay passed along by word of mouth, which is often nothing more than propaganda spread through biased sources. Such a biased source may be a government in cahoots with the media determined to achieve their objectives. They feed people information, but it is often false or misleading information, which makes society unhealthy due to its glutinous consumption of lies and deceptions. But a lie is a lie even if everyone believes it, and the truth is the truth even if no one believes it.

We live in a society filled with prejudices and bigotry despite how vigorously people try to ignore that fact by pretending that these realities don't exist. We claim that America is the greatest country on Earth because of our freedoms, but then hypocritically criticize those who utilize their rights or religious freedoms, if their beliefs are contrary to beliefs held by the "popular majority". But to which popular majority are we referring?

Should the beliefs held by the popular majority of non-Muslims who believe that all Muslims support terroristic ideologies override the beliefs held by the popular majority of practicing Muslims that say they do not condone terroristic ideologies? Should the beliefs held by one popular majority, that has limited experience or knowledge of a subject, be more accepted as truth than the beliefs held by another popular majority that has extensive experience and knowledge of that subject? Of course not!

The "popular majority" of all Muslims say that Islam does not condone any form of terrorism whatsoever. So, shouldn't the words of

Muslims who live Islam everyday carry more weight than a group of non-Muslims who think otherwise? Muslims abide by the same message given to the Children of Israel in the Qur'an:

We ordained for the Children of Israel that, if anyone killed a person—unless it be for murder or for spreading evil in the land— it would be as if he killed the whole people; and, if anyone saved a life, it would be as if he saved the lives of the whole people. Then although there came to them Our messengers with clear Signs, yet even after that, many of them continued to commit excesses in the land.

Surah Al-Maeda 5: 32

If you read the verse above and don't see the very obvious message that is being conveyed –which is, *"If you kill one life, it's as if you have killed all of humankind, and if you save one life it's as if you have saved all of humankind, in the sight of God"* and *"Some will be exposed to the truth but will ignore it"*— then you are either unable to comprehend basic English, or you stubbornly refuse to accept anything other than the opinion that you already possess. If that is the case, then honestly consider how your opinion was manufactured if you have not gone directly to the proper source in order to obtain accurate information.

There are some who simply refuse to open themselves up, even temporarily, to hearing other views or beliefs. They rely on hearsay while clinging to what is comfortable, and then adjoin themselves with other people or sources that coincide with their beliefs, while condemning those who believe differently. That type of irrationality is widespread because false information is all too often manufactured and distributed by government and media sources that have agendas that they intend to meet no matter what the cost. Then that information is twisted and distorted even further in the cesspool of social media due to fears that are invoked by strategically placed propaganda.

The reality is that we are so continuously bombarded by inaccurate and prejudiced information that people begin to believe things without seeking legitimate knowledge for themselves. That is because most people are so preoccupied with life that they simply don't have time to research for themselves, or they do not care enough to take time to seek out the truth. They ignorantly base their opinions on nothing more than hearsay and word of mouth. We should all respect one another's freedom of choice and opinion, but an opinion which is supported by a foundation of ignorance doesn't stand up to logic.

For many, it is easier to rely on hearsay than it is to take time out of their busy and sometimes not-so-busy lives in order to do study and research. Hearsay is often easily accepted and misinterpreted as facts, when it may be a watered-down version of the truth, or a version that has been grossly and purposely distorted, making it absolute false information that is injected into the veins of our society like poison.

If you are willing to open your mind, and can set aside preconceived notions, as well as the questionable popular beliefs held by the masses, you may realize that things aren't always as they appear. This should be considered by those who tend to rely on sources of information that are routinely dispersed upon the masses, which causes the majority to believe and readily accept that whatever is presented to them is legitimate truth. Such is the case with derogatory views and lies about Islam.

There are views that people swear by, without possessing true knowledge and understanding; therefore, they are lost in the fog of ignorance and delusion. It is my objective to clarify these misunderstandings to the best of my ability by presenting the truth as I know it as simply as possible and to encourage people to study and do research before accepting any information as legitimate. That means that you should research the information that I provide as well. Each individual should make effort to ensure that the information that he or she is receiving is truthful. To do that, one needs to gather information from various sources, while considering the source itself. Doing so will give you a broader understanding of the topic, which will allow you to come to your own conclusion objectively, free from biased external influence. That is what I am asking you to do with Islam. Seek the truth.

Islam, which means "submission to the will of God", is not a religion. It is a way of life. We all submit to the will of Allah, but some do it willingly as best we can while striving against our own weaknesses and inclinations (true meaning of *Jihad*), and some don't try very hard at all. But still, we all submit. That means that every human, as well as all of creation, submits to His will. Let me explain.

Religion is a man-made term. So, the "religion" of Islam did not exist when, by the will of Our Creator, He created Adam and Eve (peace be upon them); but, the "Way of Life" did, because it was only by His will that they had life. Nor did Christianity, Judaism, or any other man-made religion exist. Yet Islam (submission to the will of God) has always existed, as evident by Prophet Adam (peace be upon him), having no say-so in choosing the time or place of his creation, and by Prophet Jesus (peace be upon him) stating:

"By myself I can do nothing; I judge only as I hear, and my judgment is just, for I seek not to please myself but him who sent me."
John 5: 30 NIV

They were in complete submission to the will of Our Creator, and, like them (peace be upon them), it is only by the will of Allah, that you and I breathe, can walk, or have sight, hearing, etc. You and I, and everyone and everything ever created are in total submission to the will of God. All His creation submits to Him constantly whether we acknowledge that fact or not. It does not matter if one calls him- or herself a Christian, Hindu, Buddhist, atheist, or Muslim, we are all living in a state of Islam. That makes us all Muslims by nature, not by choice. Those who choose to follow Islam are Mu'min (true believers), and for them/us there is a great reward in this life and in the next.

No man or woman can pick and choose the days that he/she will be born or die, or who his/her parents will be, what race or gender he/she will be, or to which nationality he/she will belong. All those choices belong to our Creator and Him alone. That means that all of God's creations are Muslim at birth, whether one chooses to accept that title or not, and despite how comfortable or uncomfortable the sound of that makes you. You don't have a choice or say-so in the matter. The sun is a Muslim. The moon is a Muslim. Every tree and plant are Muslim. Every animal is Muslim. Every human being is Muslim. I am Muslim. And yes, you are Muslim!

Even a single blade of grass is in a constant state of Islam (submission) as it cries out to Allah for sustenance from the nutrients that exist in the soil of the earth, and sunlight and rain from the skies, so it too is a Muslim. My stating that you are a Muslim may be hard to comprehend and may even offend you, but I pray that by the end of this book, you will have a better and more complete understanding of what being a Muslim means and a clear understanding of what Islam is and what it is not, Insha Allah (God willing). For even the Bible says:

"Thou, even thou, art LORD alone; thou hast made heaven, the heaven of heavens, with all their host, the earth, and all things that are therein, the seas, and all that is therein, and thou preservest them all; and the host of heaven worship thee."

Nehemiah 9: 6 KJV

For those that refuse to accept or for those who are incapable of understanding this concept, I urge you to consider a verse from the Qur'an which states:

"As for those who reject faith, it is the same to them whether you warn them or do not warn them; they will not believe."

Surah Al-Baqarah 2 :6

31

What you do with the information that you receive is between you and God. My intention is not to convert you, despite the false belief that Muslims are out to convert everyone. My goal is to live up to my obligation as a Muslim, in order to persuade you into merely considering Islam for the beauty that it possesses, regardless of your inclinations towards "reverting" or not. I ask you to consider Islam logically based on truth and flee from lies and falsehood.

I use the word *revert* instead of *convert* because we are born into a natural state of Islam (submission to God's will), so we revert back to what is instinctively born within us. To move away from that natural state at birth is an unnatural conversion which is brought about by what is learned during our lifetimes, stemming from external influences; such as, parents, teachers, friends, preachers, etc. A prime example of this is the concept of "original sin". Christians believe that people are born into sin because it is commonly said that we inherit the sins of Adam (peace be upon him) when we are born, even though the Bible plainly teaches that sin is not inherited:

"The son shall not bear the iniquity of the father"
Ezekiel 18: 20 KJV

"So, then every one of us shall give account of himself to God."
Romans 14: 12 KJV

People are prone to rely more upon traditional hearsay in lieu of searching out the truth for themselves. These traditional, learned beliefs are usually passed down from generation to generation, so if your parents and grandparents are Catholic and they pray to the Virgin Mary (peace be upon her), and they call their priest "Father", which is against what the Bible teaches, then most likely that is what you grow to believe and do, even despite what the Scriptures say.

There are some who follow the Bible as Catholics that refer to priests as "Fathers", while there are others who follow the Bible as Protestant Christians, who would never do such a thing. It all depends on what you have been taught and/or exposed to. Both groups, as well as many others, interpret things differently, and therefore attempt to justify their various opinions, even though the Scriptures say:

"And call no man your father upon the earth: for one is your Father, which is in heaven."

Matthew 23: 9 KJV

Both sides can't be right, so the result is Christianity contradicting Christianity. Some accept the Catholic Bible which is comprised of seventy-three Books, while the Protestants have thrown out seven of those Books, reducing their version of the Bible to sixty-six books. We then have followers from both sides adhering to their respective traditions, based on the company they keep.

These are just a couple of the numerous examples that demonstrate how people simply accept things by tradition, peer pressure, and propaganda instead of thinking and utilizing logic for themselves. This is the type of thinking that leads one to believe that Muslims are looking to force them into being Muslim, without ever witnessing such an attempt taking place for themselves or ever hearing about it happening in the lives of someone that they know personally.

I often use the example of being the coach of a football team and foolishly trying to force someone to play on your team. It may be that, not only does that individual not want to play on your team, but also, they may not want to play the game at all!

Although one can be influenced by habitual and systematic exposure to something, one can't be forced to sincerely believe or do anything. That is especially true when it comes to religion. So why would anyone try to accomplish such an impossible task such as forcing someone to accept a religion or ideology? What good does it do for your team to have someone playing for you that is not putting his/her heart or best effort into it? You would be setting yourself up for failure and would eventually lose. It is unrealistic to think that anyone has plans to force you to accept Islam, even though you are already a Muslim. You just haven't realized it yet.

We are all Muslims because we are vulnerable in that everything happens, or nothing happens, but by the will of Allah (blessed and exalted is He). We are all constantly and forever at the mercy of, Our Creator, and what His will is for our lives. No one else has a say-so in the matter, because it is up to each individual to accept or reject the will of God in his or her life and to submit to Him alone, in obedience to His commandments and warnings.

No one can make you do that. Submission is done through sincerity and humble effort and not through coercion or threats from anyone or any group that is incapable of gauging your true intentions. The Glorious Qur'an speaks of this very issue when Allah says:

"Let there be no coercion in religion. Truth stands out clear from error. Whoever rejects evil and believes in Allah has grasped the most trustworthy grip that never breaks. And Allah hears and knows all things."

Surah Al-Baqarah 2: 256

I have purposely mentioned this verse of the Qur'an again as a prime indicator and reinforcement of the fact that, contrary to popular belief, Muslims are not out trying to force you to do anything. So, you can stop believing the never-ending nonsense being forced down your throat, so that you can logically consider what you have experienced for yourself, instead of allowing others to dictate your thinking with their hate filled rhetoric.

Now ask yourself if anyone has ever approached you or someone that you know saying, "You are going to be a Muslim, or you die!" I will answer for you, NO! Have you ever heard of such an unrealistic thing happening to anyone, other than on news broadcasts that you are incapable of verifying to be true? Absolutely..... NOT! Because no one can force you to be the Muslim that you already are. You are one who submits to the will of God, like it or not. If Jesus (peace be upon him) could do nothing in and of himself, then what makes you think you can?

You don't have to profess to be a Muslim in order to be one, and not everyone that does profess him- or herself to be a Muslim is a true believer (Mu'min) with faith firmly established in the heart. So, you can relax. The Muslims aren't plotting and planning to take over and to make you a "MOSLEM" or "MOHAMMADIAN" or a member of ISIS, and no one is going to force women to take off the revealing outfits that are so easily accepted by society to don hijabs or burkas, which promote modesty and chastity. No one is going to take the pork off your table, the alcohol out of your refrigerator, or take the nicotine and other drugs away from you. Those are choices that only you can make, so those issues are between you and our Creator. But, as a Muslim, I am going to speak the truth to you, to the Glory of and by the will of Allah (blessed and exalted is He).

Once again, what you do with the information that you receive is between you and God. But I implore you to ponder and consider what you are presented logically and to realize that you are vulnerable and always dependent on what Allah (blessed and exalted is He) provides you with, no matter what you have accomplished in this life.

If Elvis Presley and Michael Jackson (may Allah show them mercy) couldn't keep themselves alive with all of the money and fame that they acquired, then we must realize that, like them and that single blade of grass constantly crying out for sustenance, we are all living in a state of Islam or submission to the will of our Creator. By recognizing that, you must eventually realize, we are all Muslims. Yes...even you!

3

The Choice is Yours

"And my advice will not profit you, even if I wish to give you good counsel, if Allah's will is to keep you astray."

Surah Hud 11: 34

We live in an age where information is readily accessible to all. The only requirement is to possess a desire to seek and access it. In seeking information to acquire knowledge, we have a duty and obligation to seek truth and to consider the sources from which that information is obtained. Lines of communication are vital, and when it breaks down, the results are often problematic and sometimes even catastrophic.

Communication among people varies in topic, and gaging the importance of such wide varieties of topics is subjective. The earliest form of mass communication began through verbal transmission or letters written on anything readily available, such as stone, wood, parchments, etc., and then sent by courier via foot or horseback. Since then, advances in the communication process have been prevalent and of utmost importance. When communication breaks down and when information is misinterpreted or misconstrued, problems are sure to arise.

If in sending a verbal communication or letter by horseback centuries ago by courier, the courier forgot, damaged, lost, or failed to communicate the message effectively either purposely or otherwise, the recipients would have received partially incorrect, entirely incorrect, or misrepresented information, which would have left those people void of the truth. The people receiving that information would have been at a great disadvantage regarding the totality of that information and the full truth of the message attempted to be conveyed. Those people would have been forced to accept and interpret the information received to the best of their ability, based on limited knowledge and understanding. If there is a problem in the communication process, the expected result should obviously be problems.

Then there is the issue of gossip and/or the problems that arise when someone receives second-hand information which is then shared over and over again in a social echo chamber with the fine details of the original message being tainted either by accident or purposely. Issues also arise when someone overhears portions of a conversation yet feel as though they know enough about the subject matter to allow for sharing it with others who may in turn take that incorrect or partially incorrect information and repeat it themselves in an ongoing cycle. Sometimes people will overhear information being conveyed like in the days of the switchboard operator who could listen in on conversations between parties after connecting them, and then purposely spread gossip to distort what was said, throughout their community, due to a dislike for one or more parties involved or for simply being one prone to spread gossip.

Since the invention of the telegraph, telephone, radio, electronic computers, and the later invention of the internet (which came about due to a series of memos written by J.C.R. Licklider of MIT in August 1962 discussing his "Galactic Network" concept of mass social interactions and networking), people have been creating and sharing information with one another on a large scale. This technological evolution has made it possible for mankind to accomplish trading through electronic commerce, information acquisition, and communication among people in various parts of the world that are likely to never meet one another in person. Technology has also allowed mankind to commit atrocities against one another, be it socially, financially, and through acts of war. All of which begins with the spreading of information.

Despite the method utilized or the intent behind sharing information, information has and will continue to be shared, and the most important thing to consider in sharing or receiving information is its accuracy. The choice to share information with honesty and integrity is up to the person(s), group(s), and/or organization(s) sharing it, and the choice to accept information received as valid, accurate, and correct is up to the individual(s) receiving it. In exchanging information with one another, people should make efforts to ensure that the information is correct for the sake of all parties involved. This is especially true when the consequence of spreading information affects masses of people in our society. This means that the process starts with the individual placing the responsibility on each person to verify what to accept or reject as truth. No one can force anyone else to do this. The choice is yours.

When presented with information of which we were not eye witnesses and/or have no legitimate way of verifying as accurate, it is only befitting and logical that each of us follow up to investigate what we have heard through known respected sources. Not doing so places people in a state of ignorance, allowing for potential manipulation by others. This is a scenario in which people will base their opinions and beliefs on bogus or inaccurate information that they may sincerely believe to be true. So, I pray that while reading this book the reader will consider this and be encouraged to investigate information that is presented while remembering that the acceptance of hearsay and/or secondhand information is not a healthy or reliable means in which to establish one's personal opinions or beliefs. The fact is, that type of information is most often inaccurate or completely wrong. Rumors beget more rumors, so secondhand information should never be trusted as legitimate and authoritative.

We all need to be cautious when taking things at face value because, like the adage says, there are two sides to every story. We always have the option to research information thoroughly and it is our responsibility to do so. No one can force you to accept or reject anything, and no one can decide for you how to decipher information. Once again, the choice is yours.

Obviously, no one likes being lied to or deceived. But the fact is that most people believe whatever they hear, and a great majority of what someone overhears is flawed. That is especially so when people hear the same flawed information repeatedly from various sources that either add or leave out details. Most people do not question things that are repeated often because repetition seems to play a major role in one's willingness to accept something as valid. Consider the following analogy: If a child is repeatedly told that Santa Clause is real, eventually that child is going to believe it to be so, especially when presented with that information by parents that are on the first line as authority figures in their lives. So, why do parents tell their children that Santa is real when it is not true? Obviously, there is a purpose and agenda behind it and that purpose is to manipulate the children into accepting what they themselves deem as important and meaningful enough that they would resort to spreading an untruth to persuade their children into accepting the celebration of an ancient pagan holiday –a celebration of which they themselves relive vicariously through their children. This process has been repeated for millennia.

After being brainwashed by the untruth, children will excitedly discuss it among themselves because they truly believe that on Christmas Day, jolly Old St. Nick will be coming to town with a bag full of toys for all of the good little girls and boys! But only if they are good and only if they believe it. Of course, the parents that involve their children in this ongoing fabricated story want them to go to sleep early so that they can set presents out around a decorated tree without being seen or discovered. With the kids being asleep and oblivious to the scheme, the parents are allotted the opportunity to proceed silently in the dark shadows of the night to accomplish their goal. The parents will go to extreme measures so as not to be discovered, in fear of the consequences of being exposed as frauds in disappointing their children.

In a similar fashion, society has been put to sleep and deceived by frauds. There are people in our world that, like the parents mentioned above, will spread known falsehoods to achieve their agendas because they feel the end justifies the means. Like the children that believe in Santa, masses of people are hoodwinked into believing lies and in many instances will unknowingly become promoters of those lies themselves, like children who go to school and discuss Santa with their classmates who, like themselves, have been fed the very same lie by their own parents as well! But the reality is, one day the lie will be discovered.

Even after the lie about Santa Clause is discovered, there are some children that will adamantly refuse to believe anything other than what they have been told all their lives. For a period, the children will be in a confused and emotional state of denial. Those children will often accuse the other children, who have discovered the lie and shared it, as being liars themselves! They will argue, cry, call names, and even fight to defend the lie that they sincerely want to be the truth. They want to believe their version of the truth because their version makes them feel good and they do not want to believe that their own parents have lied to them. The choice to believe or not believe is up to the individual, and like them, the choice is yours.

Now ponder and reflect on the following questions. Have you ever believed in Santa? Do you know of someone that presently believes in Santa or who has in the past? Do you know or have you ever known someone who has, or currently persuades others to believe, that Santa exists? Have you ever seen someone pose as Santa Claus in a shopping mall while parents of naïve and excitedly deceived and nervous children bring them to further enforce and solidify the lie by having them meet one of the imposters face-to-face while awkwardly embraced in his lap?

Now ask yourself; who is the greater deceiver in this lie? Is it the mall personnel who hired the costumed character of chicanery, giving him a platform in which to perform his trickery? Is it the parents that took advantage of the opportunity to further deceive their children into believing their lie? Or is it the bearded one himself that dons the attire to reap financial gain or to perversely gain access to the children because he is aroused by the emotional responses that his presence invokes, be they good or bad? What about the other patrons of the mall that watch from a distance while being entertained by the campaign of deception, although not directly involved in it?

Now let's consider the example of the ongoing deception about Santa Clause as we consider Islam. For comparison, let's use the analogy of producing a movie titled "The Choice is Yours". For illustrative purposes, the actors involved in this example will be replaced below. The genre of this story is defined in many terms -- drama, action, adventure, fiction, animated, CGI, fantasy, horror, thriller, comedy, religious, and, yes, even romance due to the way people embrace and react to such things with great passion and emotion.

Cast

Directors/Writers – Represents government officials looking to accomplish a specific goal.

Mall – Represents the news and/or social media which creates and promotes the platform.

Parents – Represents Islamophobes or those that are looking to persuade others towards fear.

Children – Represents those in society who can choose to accept or reject the information and those that are constantly being molded by information absorbed during one's lifetime.

Mall Patrons – Represents those being entertained by the actions of others but who will join in on the shenanigans from time to time.

Extras – Represents those in society that play a variety of roles.

Villains – Represents those who purposely spread hatred by distorting the truth.

Muslims – Represents the so-called villains that have been targeted by the Writers/Directors.

I ask the reader of this book to separate yourself from any presuppositions or beliefs that you may have about Islam and to consider issues presented honestly and without bias. Keep in mind that the truth is the truth even if no one believes it, and a lie is a lie even if everyone believes it. The choice is yours as to what to accept or reject.

As with the fictional story about Santa Clause, there have been things said about Islam which have been purposely distorted with the intent to persuade the masses into believing that Islam is something that it is not, while denying what it is. Like children who have been told that Santa Claus is coming to town, people all over the world have been led to believe that Muslims are coming to take over. Yes, children have seen so-called Santa Claus figures in malls, cartoons, on post cards, etc. all over the world, but seeing those images and imposters posing as Santa does not mean that Santa Claus is real. On the contrary, the only thing real about Santa Claus is the lie that has been propagated about him for generations. In the same manner, members of ISIS and other terrorist groups have been presented as ambassadors of Islam all over the world, through the spreading of false information by hate mongers looking to instill fear in society.

In 1991, the FBI supposedly came across a document by the "Muslim Brotherhood" titled *Explanatory Memorandum*. Afterwards, former federal prosecutor and writer for *National Review* and author of the book *The Grand Jihad, Andrew McCarthy,* spoke about the document saying: "Islamic supremacists mean us grave harm. We are understandably preoccupied with the fact that violent Jihadists are taking aim at our lives, but we should not let the immediacy and horrors of that threat obscure the fact that the Islamist Movement is taking aim at our way of life, and the movement's intellectual leaders is the Muslims Brotherhood."

The purpose of that statement was to draw attention to, not only a physical threat by this Muslim Brotherhood group, but also to imply that a silent and passive "Jihad" was taking place as well. People were led to believe that Muslims were attacking on all fronts in all out warfare, even though the only signs of those attacks were in news broadcasts. This type of psychological warfare is used to attract, misinform, and anesthetize the brain into believing something that is not true, like color imagery used by food establishments. Through this imagery, people become convinced that they are hungry. This tactic is not used to inform, but to inflame. It is not to enlighten but to deceive through systematic rhetoric which is consistently aimed at the target audience to not only gain approval, but also to develop and manufacture consent to the degree that common people become promoters of the cause with an attitude of patriotism and loyalty.

That sense of loyalty leads people to feel that the cause is just and to take a position of defense, just like the children that believe Santa is coming. It causes people to believe that there is an imminent danger and therefore a call to arms is necessary. So, people take up arms against a threat that they have not seen or experienced for themselves. It's like being told by word of mouth or overhearing that a storm is coming but never stopping to check the radar, consult a news broadcast, or even look outside to verify it for yourself. Sure, there very well may be a potential storm on the way, but did you personally hear the meteorologist say where it is forecast to hit? The forecast may predict an 80% chance of rainfall, but you may not see a single drop of rain! You can don your raingear and grab your umbrella for fear of getting wet, but unless you heard that the storm was forecast to hit your area, you would be jumping to a conclusion that can only be deemed as irrational. If you base your decision to walk around in rainboots and a slicker suit all day based on limited information about a storm that may not even be heading your way, you would be demonstrating signs of paranoia and/or irrational logic. If you rely upon information about a storm from someone who is not an authority or who may be passing on information that they themselves overheard, then you would be relying on unreliable information. So, consider your options. You can accept what you "heard" blindly, or you can wisely investigate the issue yourself from a reliable and dependable source. The choice is yours.

As in the example of children believing in Santa, the emotions of people have been preyed upon, causing them to believe that Muslims are contemplating their demise. Use of the vague title "Muslim Brotherhood" generates the belief for some people that all Muslims are or will eventually be members of that organization. It is through blanket phrases such as this that people are grouped together and labeled. Additionally, stereotypes are developed, and people are branded for things that they have not done, by people that have not seen those things occur for themselves. All of which has been generated through the spreading of information that we have a responsibility to verify. No one can make you seek the truth, nor can anyone force you to accept Islam. The choice is yours.

"Let there be no coercion in religion. Truth has been made clear from error."

Surah Al Baqarah 2: 148

4
Patriots of Propaganda

"[Propaganda] must be aimed at the emotions and only to a very limited degree at the so-called intellect... The art of propaganda lies in understanding the emotional ideas of the great masses and finding, through a psychologically correct form, the way to the attention and thence to the heart of the broad masses."

Adolph Hitler
(Adolf Hitler (1998), "Mein Kampf", Houghton Mifflin Harcourt)

Has anyone ever approached you or anyone that you know, attempting to force you to accept Islam? I am more than confident that the answer is, No! Yet we live in a society in which people have been systematically led to believe that this type of interaction has occurred in the past, does occur presently, or may eventually take place at some point in the future. This type of thinking falls into the category of a "phobia" or "Islamophobia" in particular.

There are people who absolutely detest being labeled with such a title, while claiming that such a word does not exist; yet, those same people display characteristics and attributes which fall right in line with proving that it does. Many of those same people expend large amounts of time and effort to discredit and attack Islam because of fear. It is common for people to admit that they have this fear of Islam, without ever being directly threatened or affected by it in any way. Those very people will admit the fear and then oddly profess that they aren't afraid in the same breath, as they fall into the logical fallacy of cognitive dissonance. They fear and admit it but then oddly deny it because they think it makes them look vulnerable or soft. It is the fear within them that generates this irrational state of mind that makes people defensive and offensive at the same time, so that the people who claim they are being attacked become the ones on the attack.

Some people irrationally fear that Muslims are conspiring to take over their way of life and to implement Sharia. We see this phenomenon occurring on various fronts in the form of subtle to obviously blatant attacks in the news media, as well as social media, being propagated by people who refuse to admit that they have this fear, while simultaneously instigating and inculcating this fear in others. Most often those people are too proud to admit that they are simply afraid. They want to believe that there is a legitimate threat that must be addressed and so they exhaust themselves using limited information and knowledge to draw attention to what they themselves have never seen or experienced personally.

"I don't believe there is such a thing as a moderate Islamist party. The challenge with Islamists is that they seek to impose what they call Sharia on everybody, Muslim and non-Muslim alike."

Frank Gaffney

Frank J. Gaffney is the Founder and President of the *Center for Security Policy* in Washington, D.C. According to the *Southern Poverty Law Center*, Gaffney believes that "Creeping Shariah," or Islamic religious law, is a dire threat to American democracy. He is an American counter-jihad conspiracy theorist.

There are others who are less combatant and far less vocal, yet still possess characteristics indicative of this unjustifiable fear. A fear manufactured in the subterfuge of the politically charged influence of the media, which utilizes a message of gradual dehumanization that resonates and echoes throughout society, thereby poisoning the minds of people against their neighbors.

Through carefully crafted schemes of chicanery by those in power, governments throughout the world position themselves as puppet masters of persuasion by using the media in controlling the masses.

These government-led stratagems of puppetry and population control are all too familiar as history has demonstrated time and time again, as one group or another is routinely and systematically singled out, branded, labeled, and targeted in vicious campaigns of hate and prejudice generated in the skullduggery of propaganda enacted against them.

"The media's the most powerful entity on earth. They have the power to make the innocent guilty and to make the guilty innocent, and that's power, because they control the minds of the masses."

Malcolm X

If you honestly consider the following definition you will see that the label "Islamophobes" is more than befitting for certain groups of people who have been caught up in the snares of this irrational obsession. The process of inciting this obsession has been covert and camouflaged behind national pride, and the movement has been constant. The consistency is the key, as people are routinely reminded of the possibility of a threat that they have never experienced themselves.

As you consider this definition, the reader should ponder and reflect on reasons why people all over the world would adhere to such beliefs and measure the irrational justifications utilized to explain their reasoning, and how this came about.

pho-bi-a (noun) an extreme or irrational fear of or aversion to something.

Ex.: He had a **phobia about** being under water."

synonyms: fear, irrational fear, obsessive fear, dread, horror, terror, hatred, loathing, detestation, aversion, antipathy, revulsion.

Now consider the following questions: Are you afraid that Muslims are conspiring to take over or to control your way of life? Do you know anyone that does feel that way? Have you seen people in the media that claim that this threat or possibility exists? Have those people influenced you in any miniscule way regarding Islam? Only you can answer the first two questions about yourself and those with whom you associate, but the likely answers to the last two questions is, "Yes".

What we see and/or hear influences us in some form or fashion and seeing and hearing people spew anti-Muslim, anti-Islam rhetoric has been an all too common occurrence.

Since 9/11, three things have become apparent throughout society.

1) Numerous misconceptions about Islam.
2) Limited levels of understanding and knowledge about Islam.
3) The existence of fear and hatred against Islam.

The continuous bombardment of attacks against Islam since 9/11 has led people to develop an all too familiar "Us vs Them" mentality, and this way of thinking has been growing and intensifying since the Trump Era began. This has been achieved using carefully crafted slogans such as, "Radical Islamic Terrorists", "Muslim Extremists", "The War on Terror", "They hate us", "Implementation of Sharia Law", and "Islam oppresses women", etc., which have been meshed into the phrase, "Muslim Fundamentalists". All of these have been magnified by the Muslim Travel Ban, implemented shortly after President Trump's inauguration.

To persuade people into believing that the fundamentals of being a "Moderate Muslim" require you to be or eventually become oppressive radical extremists, these slogans have been repeated over and over again influencing masses of people and causing them to sincerely believe that being Muslim correlates to being terrorists. This campaign of prejudice and fear has been tactfully propagated behind a veil of lies and misconceptions which have led people to accept and believe things about Islam that simply are not true.

My synopsis is that this effort constitutes as hate mongering and prejudice being propagated under the guise of patriotism, hidden behind the veils of "Homeland Security". Even though these attacks against Islam are obviously apparent and continuing to intensify, people turn a blind eye to them because they feel that their hatred and views are justified, and this diluted way of thinking is all a part of the plan.

"We have seen a politics of fear used to justify discrimination against Muslims. This has resulted in unwarranted surveillance, unlawful profiling, and exclusionary immigration policies targeting people based on their faith, nationality, or national origin. Such discriminatory policies have been accompanied by a worrying rise in hateful rhetoric, which has severe consequences. At a time when hate crimes are down overall, they are up against American Muslims."

American Civil Liberties Union (www.aclu.org) under the title,
Anti-Muslim Discrimination

To gain public approval, this campaign of slanderous accusations and fear has been used by political Islamophobes and shot callers with the purpose of converting common everyday people into consistent everyday Islamophobes. Common everyday people are either blind to this phenomenon or simply too proud to admit that they have been seduced by propaganda and the subliminal messages that have been used to control their thinking and emotions. This type of social warfare is not new, as it has been used time and time again by people of power looking to achieve their agendas, while seeking the support of the common people to succeed. In the process of these campaigns, the media is used to excite the thinking and emotions of the people in instituting a sense of national pride, which makes them feel that the cause is just and that the threat is against everyone. That so-called "threat" for Islamophobes is Islam, and so we have seen a gradual paradigm shift in society which has replaced the "enemy over there" attitude with "The enemies in our midst" attitude.

"The purpose of propaganda is not to provide interesting distraction for blasé young gentlemen, but to convince... the masses. But the masses are slow moving, and they always require a certain time before they are ready even to notice a thing, and only after the simplest ideas are repeated thousands of times will the masses finally remember them."

Adolph Hitler
(Adolf Hitler (1998), "Mein Kampf", Houghton Mifflin Harcourt)

We see examples of these campaigns of hate when we reflect on history and consider the atrocities enacted against various groups and/or races of people such as Native Americans, Jewish people during the Holocaust, Japanese Americans during World War II, the enslavement of Africans, and the ongoing racism enacted against their African American descendants during the Jim Crow Era, as well as now. Most recently, the attacks have been against those that "appear" to be of Arab/Muslim descent, simply because they look like the stereotypical idea of "terrorists" as portrayed in the media. The residual damage generated by the atrocities of 9/11 has been inflicted on people who had nothing to do with the attacks and who vehemently disapprove of the actions committed by only nineteen people, because they look like them.

Those nineteen murderers are known to have spent the night before the attacks visiting strip clubs and consuming alcohol which are both strictly forbidden in Islam. Yet despite their actions, which are inconsistent with Islamic teachings, they have been associated with Islam and through vicarious liability, anyone that looks like they did or who call themselves Muslims, have been branded as terrorists or potential terrorists themselves. We have seen this occurring due to the racial profiling of people that may or may not be Muslims at all. In many instances, people of other religions as well as atheists have been targeted unjustly simply due to their appearance, and of course true Muslims have been targeted while completely innocent.

In each one of these instances where previous groups were conspired against, we see the common man being systematically brainwashed into thinking that those people were subhuman and not worthy of life, let alone deserving of respect and basic human rights. As history repeats itself, we see this as being the case with Muslims in the world today.

Routinely throughout history, whole masses of people have been targeted and labeled as the "problem" and then attacked on numerous fronts by their antagonists who operate with a political motive to lead the common citizen into believing that their cause is just. Due to this influence, common everyday people become patriots of propaganda on a united front against perceived or so-called enemies. History has demonstrated that this will even pit neighbor against neighbor at times, because people are made to feel that the enemy is so close that they are closing in and lurking right outside, as social paranoia sets in.

During a speech by Pulitzer Prize winning Religious and Historical Author Gary Wills, author of the book *What the Qur'an Meant (Why it Matters)*, he made the following comment:

"What the hell is the 'Sharia' they are condemning and how is it going to sneak up on us? Is it one of the four Sunni Sharia Laws or is it the three Shia? Of course, they have no idea because they don't know anything about what they are condemning. What they are doing is saying, 'My God they hate us! They're sneaking up on us!' It's like our good Anti-Communist days when there was a Communist.... Communism was going to infiltrate our government. There was a Communist under the bed. Well, now there are Muslims under the bed."

In the efforts to secure the support of the people, many tactics are utilized, blinding people to the ways in which they have been influenced. Ironically, many will completely deny the possibility that this effort to persuade them could even exist or ever be effective. They are blinded by a false sense of independence and are oblivious to the ways in which they have been influenced and manipulated by population control.

When Muslims attempt to tell the truth about Islam, they are often shut down with a word used by the Islamophobes as a mental wall – "Taqiyya!" The word *taqiyya* is defined as "lying" by those using it to attack Muslims, but that is another misrepresentation of Islam. It is used to claim that Islam allows Muslims to lie about anything. During the 2016 presidential race, candidate Dr. Ben Carson said that the Islamic doctrine of taqiyya encourages Muslims "to lie to achieve your goals". That statement prompted Washington Post's Glenn Kessler to quote a number of academics to show that the presidential candidate got it wrong.

The word *taqiyya* is related to the Arabic word for piety, which is *taqwah*. Its root means to protect or guard oneself against evil while maintaining a conscious and healthy fear of God. It means to guard yourself against the wrath of Allah (blessed and exalted is He). It also means to use logical self-preservation against religious persecution.

A verse in the Qur'an was revealed on topic of taqiyya. It relates to the torture and religious persecution against the family of Ammaar ibn Yasir (may Allah be pleased with him). His parents were the first martyrs in Islam. His mother Sammayah (may Allah be pleased with her) was killed by Abu Jahl who hated Islam. He ran a spear through her belly. The father was then tortured and killed. Ammar witnessed the murders of both his parents. Finally, Ammar himself was tortured repeatedly as he was forced to lie on scorching hot, rocky ground and then endure having heavy rocks piled on his chest and abdomen. Boiling water was poured on him as he was demanded to deny Islam and condemn Prophet Muhammed (peace be upon him).

At times, Ammar gave in to the torture and verbally rejected Islam and Prophet Muhammed, but he would later repent. He was obviously under mental, emotional, and physical duress. When Ammar told Prophet Muhammed (peace be upon him) about the verbal rejections, the Prophet asked, "How do you feel in your heart?" Ammar replied, "I feel my heart is content in faith." The Prophet told him, "If they do so again, you do the same." After that, the following verse was revealed:

"It is only those who do not believe in the verses of Allah who fabricate falsehood, and it is they who are liars. If a person accepts faith in Allah and then, afterward, states unbelief, he may do so under coercion but really remain firm in faith in his heart. If he disbelieves in his heart, then the wrath of Allah will be upon that person. A horrible penalty will come upon such people."
Surah An-Nahl 16: 105-106

Our Creator addresses the issue again:

"Do not allow the believers to take unbelievers as supporters instead of believers. Whoever does that will never be helped by Allah in any way –unless there is fear of danger from them. Allah warns you against Himself, and to Allah is the final return. Say, 'Whether you hid what is in your breasts or reveal it, Allah knows it, and He knows what is in the heavens and what is in the earth. And Allah is able to do all things.'"
Surah Al-Imran 3: 28-29

Obviously, only our Creator can judge the intentions and sincerity of one's heart. Just as it is impossible to force someone to sincerely accept something or someone, it is equally impossible to fore someone to reject something or someone. Although Ammar made a verbal declaration in rejecting Islam and Prophet Muhammed (peace be upon him), he did not feel that way in his heart. While he did indeed lie to his enemies in order to save himself, his devotion to Islam and the Prophet remained intact.

To prevent torture and death is one of only three reasons for which taqiyya may be used. Another reason is when a false compliment is better than a hurtful truth; for example, if a woman asks her husband, "How do I look in this outfit?", it is better that he responds, "Like the most beautiful woman in the world," even if it is not be true.

The third example of using taqiyya is when a harmonious situation needs to be set up in order to assist reconciliation between two feuding parties. In this situation, one would tell Party A that Party B wants to discuss peace, and then one would tell Party B that Party A wants to discuss peace, when it may be that neither party wants to discuss peace. It is better to arrange this amicable situation by use of taqiyya than it is to do nothing to rectify the situation.

Contrary to what the Muslim-haters claim, taqiyya cannot be used to cover up anything non-Muslims find objectionable in Islam. For example, a Muslim cannot claim that Islam recognizes that Jesus' "sacrifice on the cross" is the path to salvation. As much as the Christians want us to say that, Muslims simply do not accept this doctrine, so we can't make them like us by agreeing with them on that. The message that many people get, however, is that Muslims may use taqiyya any way necessary to hide truths about Islam and make it more attractive.

The mass movement and implantation of ideologies and beliefs in society is and always has been prominent in pushing people in one direction or another, and awareness of such campaigns is paramount. Until we begin to recognize this influence by those in power over us, we will never be able to free ourselves from their manipulations.

"Propaganda works best when the people being manipulated are confident, they are acting on their own free will."

Paul Joseph Goebbels
(Chancellor of Nazi Germany)

Paul Joseph Goebbels was a German Nazi politician and Reich Minister of Propaganda of Nazi Germany from 1933 to 1945. He was one of Adolf Hitler's closest advisors and followers. The use of propaganda was perfected by Nazi Germany against their Jewish peoples and their tactics have been well studied and repeated. Due to modern technology and the rapid spread of information via the internet, it is obvious that no other group of people has been attacked as relentlessly and consistently as Muslims have been. The onslaught against Muslims in the news media has been magnified in social media by people that ignorantly repeat what they have heard others say without having true knowledge about what they are discussing. The hatred and ridicule are prominent and unmistakable as the snowball effect has grown and been targeted at Islam.

This vicious cycle has been socially destructive, and it seems that lines have been drawn in the sand using divisive slogans such as the one below, which doesn't leave any option but to side with one group against another. Nor does it define who the "terrorists" are, leaving people to interpret who those people are for themselves. So, we must ask, who is former President Bush talking about?

"You are either with us, or you are with the terrorists."

George W. Bush
(Former President of the United States)

In the past visual aids were utilized to instill fear and hatred in people. After the Japanese Kamikaze attacks on Pearl Harbor, posters such as the well-known "This is the Enemy" posters were created and dispersed on a mass scale depicting a yellow monkey with slanted eyes and holding a knife. The image was supposed to be of a Japanese soldier attempting to attack a defenseless and hysterical Caucasian woman from behind. The woman used to depict the stereotypical idea of beauty in the United States, had a peach colored skin tone with no animalistic traits, unlike the other star of the popular poster. This form of psychological warfare caused people to hate all Japanese peoples. The animalistic depiction of the so-called Japanese soldier was utilized to dehumanize and disassociate him with the woman as being human. A similar tactic was used against Jewish people during World War II, as so-called Jewish people were depicted on posters with oversized facial features.

Many of those posters were entitled "He is responsible for the war". In that depiction, German propagandists were attempting to imply that the very people being victimized by genocide were responsible for their own victimization! Shockingly, the common German peoples began to believe it, so neighbor attacked and plotted against neighbor in an effort to eradicate the Jewish people from the face of the Earth. The German people saw themselves as superior, and they did not want their pure bloodlines to be "tainted". They were trained to believe that their Jewish neighbors were the root cause of all social problems in their society and that eliminating them would solve the problems. History demonstrates that this has been a common tactic used against the various groups that I have mentioned earlier in this chapter, and we see history repeating itself once again regarding Muslims and the religion of Islam.

"If you are not careful, the newspapers will have you hating the people that are being oppressed, and loving the people that are doing the oppressing"

Malcolm X

As with prior groups of people that have been targeted throughout history through the process of dehumanization, many people truly believe that Islam is evil and that it promotes violence, oppression, the subjugation of women, as well as death for those who oppose or leave Islam. These beliefs are derived from falsehoods which are attributed to Islam and then propagated and promoted to the common man in society, who then accepts what he has heard without looking into the issues for himself. Looking into these vital issues requires time and effort that most people don't have to spend or utilize, simply because they are too busy trying to provide for their families and dealing with life. It is also possible that they simply do not have the desire to delve into research about a foreign and often not so foreign people and/or religion that they can't relate to. They feel it has nothing to do with their lives.

That mentality is extremely hypocritical because many of these same people will justify and base their beliefs purely on, "hearsay", while under the false impression that these issues, that they ironically don't feel are important enough to investigate themselves, are bound to disrupt their way of life at some point, even to the point of death! On one hand the issues aren't important enough to sincerely investigate, but on the other, they are somehow important enough to generate hate, fear, and the physical, mental, and emotional subjugation of others.

The cacophony of this hate and fear is booming loud and clear by people who are quick to voice their opinions boisterously and passionately, based on very limited knowledge about what they are discussing. Those misinformed people are influenced by so-called experts in the field, who are paid large sums of money to engage in hijacking Islam through speeches, guest appearances on talk shows, and news broadcasts. Those people will be addressed in the next chapter.

Many of those people claim to be ex-Muslims who have a firsthand experience with Islam, yet many can't tell you what the five pillars of Islam are. Despite that, those people are consulted and used to attack Islam. They claim that Islam is an evil and false religion that is oppressive to all non-believers and Muslim women. Contrary to popular belief, Muslim women are honored in Islam. Oppression of any kind is not allowed in Islam, and that fact is indicated by the following verse of the Holy Qur'an where our Creator says:

Kenny Bomer

"We will reserve the houses of the hereafter exclusively for those who do not seek self-glory in this life and do not cause oppression and corruption to spread. The final outcome belongs to those who fear."

Surah Al-Qasas 28: 83

The branding and labeling of Islam and Muslims as evil is achieved using propaganda that is more prominent now than in any other time in the history of the world. The avenues to disperse false information has grown exponentially, and the acceptance of this information as a form of entertainment is more than evident as people routinely discover information quicker on social media than they do in relying on news broadcasts like people in the past. This allows for sharing of false information by people who most often spend a mere matter of seconds flipping through various things on their smart phones as a form of their own personal entertainment. The unfortunate thing is that it only takes seconds to lead someone astray.

When people see a certain slogan or headline, often enough they are prone to accept it without ever stopping to read the article itself. The slogans that are fired in rapid succession throughout the radio, television, movies, news media, and social media are propaganda at its finest. Attack from all sides suddenly and relentlessly! Blitzkrieg!

"But the most brilliant propogandist technique will yield no success unless one fundamental principle is borne in mind constantly and with unflagging attention. It must confine itself to a few points and repeat them over and over. Here, as so often in this world, persistence is the first and most important requirement for success."

Adolph Hitler
(Adolf Hitler (1998), "Mein Kampf," Houghton Mifflin Harcourt)

5
War of the Worlds

Fake news! What qualifies as "fake news" seems to be difficult to decipher and discern in modern times. Especially since the onset of the "Trump Era" in which network has been pitted against network, and once well-respected news organizations have been equated to tabloids. This calls to mind the old idioms, "Seeing is believing" and "I will believe it when I see it". But the challenge comes when what you think you see is a mere mirage causing you to believe in something that isn't real. The potential mirage in the news world is the headlines which are perpetuated by propagators of politically inspired propaganda as they push to persuade whole masses of people while perpetrating their frauds, as mentioned in the previous chapters.

"Whoever controls the media, controls the mind."

Jim Morrison

We live in an age in which people have access to news quicker than in the past. Social Media provides an abundance of information to the world allowing people instant access to whatever is transpiring in real time, so people no longer need to rely on their local or national news broadcasts to get information on current events. Nowadays, people routinely record happenings on their smartphones going "live" or will post recordings of events, allowing news to spread very rapidly. But the news organizations are still recognized as the authorities in explaining what is being seen with their "Breaking News" broadcasts and associated headlines, as well as ongoing analysis that transpires afterwards.

The unfortunate thing is that the "analysis" usually differs between one news organization and another as they battle back and forth with differing "left" and "right" views. Society is left not knowing what is right and not knowing what to believe or not believe! The reality is that people are generally prone to lean toward the side that seems to be in tune with their beliefs and ideas. FOX News seems to support Donald Trump while CNN is seen as attacking him. Whose version of the so-called "truth" is correct, if either? The issue is compounded when people on social media begin to interpret what they have been presented and then proceed to put their personal spin on the issues as it all spirals out of control leaving the world in absolute confusion with people being at odds with one another.

Poison is spread, and minds are either adversely sedated or stimulated by the injections of political influence on the media, whose credibility has come under fire, due to the President of the United States consistently utilizing the phrase "fake news". This phrase, which was originally invented by Adolph Hitler, was used to make excuses for Hitler's unethical behavior and to undermine the media when exposing him. It is used by Trump for the same purpose in current times.

The same man that seems to support "Freedom of the Press" when attacking others or when congratulating himself for some self-aggrandized achievement, has attempted to discredit the press when they reveal issues that expose him. One side will see him as an innocent sheep being led to slaughter, while the other sees him as the "Big Bad Wolf" out to devour as many sheep as possible. Regardless of varying perceptions, there is an "Elephant in the Room" and the size of that elephant dictates the outcome of what is portrayed in the media.

In a matter of decades, the world has gone from a point of total reliance upon the media as trusted and respected sources of information, to not being able to completely trust any of those sources. An example of this is the so-called "Resistance Letter" published by the New York Times on Wednesday September 4, 2018. It was supposedly written by an anonymous writer identified only as a

"Senior Official in the Trump Administration". It suggested that the so-called "good guys" were aware of the bad guy" and that they were working in the shadows to address his actions in order to protect the people of the United States. The nation was left to decide whether or not the letter was indeed written by a member of the Trump Administration or someone else conspiring against his administration from the outside. So, who is the wolf and who is the sheep in that situation, and does it really matter when the elephant is carrying the weight? What if the weight is a smoke screen of confusion meant to cause people in society to question and argue about what the truth is, as a premeditated diversion tactic used to draw attention away from the bigger plot or scheme?

Could it be that the purpose was to have people talking about and looking for the "mole" in the White House, whose actions could be deemed as treasonous, in order to take emphasis off the acts committed by Trump that could justify impeachment? Could it be that the purpose of this modern-day propaganda is to leave people not knowing what to believe or not believe so that when evil is committed it can be covered up as if the act committed didn't really happen at all? Either way, the issue that is most prevalent regarding that anonymous letter is that the public does not know what to believe or who to trust as each side claims to be the true patriots of the people, and vice versa, in this ongoing war of political propaganda.

"The people can always be brought to the bidding of the leaders...tell them they are being attacked and denounce the peacemakers for lack of patriotism and exposing the country to danger."

Herman Goring
(Quoted in Gustave M. Gilbert, Nuremberg Diary 1947)

Have you ever heard a song playing on the radio for the very first time, and you did not initially care for it, but then after hearing it played repeatedly, you eventually memorized the lyrics, and grew to like it while singing along and possibly dancing to it? I think we have all experienced something like that in our lives. This is a process of the changing of the mind which is described in theories of learning in psychology as, *Classical Conditioning*, or more precisely, *Conditioned Stimulus* and *Conditioned Reflex*, as studied by Russian Psychologist, Ivan Pavlov (Father of Classical Conditioning).

In the music business there is a common term called "the hook", which describes the part of a song, usually the chorus, which people remember most. Often people begin singing the "hook" of the song the very first time that they hear the song, before it has ended. It is usually a catchy phrase that people latch onto and remember after the song has ended. What this demonstrates is the residual effect on people when presented with something repeatedly. Over time people will eventually develop a willingness to accept what is presented despite their initial thoughts or feelings.

This also occurs in the reverse fashion when rejecting something that was once accepted. Sometimes opinions change without people recognizing that the transformation occurred and without understanding or consideration being made as to why? It just happens.... or so it seems.

We must become ever more aware of the gradual, yet consistent, conditioning and reconditioning of the mind, taking place in our society. Conditioning and reconditioning which is utilized to put people in a mind-state of acceptance towards the support or rejection of something, someone, or even an ideology. To fully grasp the understanding of this concept, you must be capable of looking beyond the shallow thinking of everyday life, to look outside of the box into the depths of the issues that we face in society, lest we fall victim to mind control.

This is a control which occurs on many different levels, by manipulating the masses and causing people to believe or disbelieve, or to accept or reject. It's a play on emotions used to manufacture certain emotions or desires, all of which is dependent upon the objective and level of successful effort by those who are seeking to sway opinions in one direction or another. A prime example of this is achieved through advertising.

Advertising is utilized in order to sway and seduce the masses into accepting the product that the manufacturer wishes to distribute. But the product being distributed isn't limited to being a material item or consumable, it can also be a belief or an idea that is being sold and/or consumed. The key to a successful advertising campaign is marketing and presentation. Marketing is a form of communication between the supplier and the target audience, with the goal of selling the product at all costs. Therefore, the presentation of the product is critical.

The goal is to convince the target audience that the product is so good that everyone needs it, even if the product is bad for you! We have seen the success of this in the examples of advertisements for cigarettes, alcohol, and "fast food". Society consumes these products despite the negative health effects that they generate. Therefore, it is obvious that the impact of advertising on society can be so strong and effective that it impacts values, which reflects the morals of society as a whole. So, we have parents consuming these products; i.e., smoking cigarettes despite the health risk while their children and others around them breathe in secondhand smoke. Or, they will eat "Big Macs" and then proceed to feed their children "Happy Meals", with very little concern for their own health, let alone the health of their children! Any concern that does exist is negated by the ease of acceptance which is reflected by the "fast food" establishments.

This is where the "value system" comes into play. Society has sacrificed logic and truth or tolerance and acceptance, throughout numerous areas of our lives. The powers of persuasion cause us to accept things that we instinctively know aren't right --things that poison society in numerous ways –physically, mentally, emotionally, and spiritually. We are rejecting what we know is right in preference for what we know is wrong.

By doing so, we are normalizing negative values and behaviors and even uplifting and glamourizing them in many instances. A prime example of this is the decades-long transformations of the movie and music industries, which have continually gotten more and more risqué, sexual, violent, and perverse. These are true reflections of our society which demonstrate how things that were once unacceptable have become common and mainstream.

It seems that society has become nonsensical and perverse, and its heart has become blackened and hardened to the point that people have lost all conscience and conviction, which means that everything is accepted, and what was once seen as immoral is now common place. This undoubtedly demonstrates that a portion of society has lost all consciousness of our Creator and that their levels of ethics are gradually diminishing, which is undoubtedly a painful reality that lies at the very heart of our society today.

It is narrated in the Hadith (sayings of the Prophet) that Prophet Muhammad (peace be upon him) said:

"Beware, in the body there is a piece of flesh; if it is sound, the whole body is sound, and if it is corrupt, the whole body is corrupt; and, hearken, it is the heart."

Sahih Muslim

What is the condition of the heart of society? There is a portion of society that seems to be lost in the darkness due to the dim lights of lies and propaganda that blind many people, causing them to lose focus on good values and to engage in behaviors that will eventually bring about the demise of society, or more precisely, the demise of intended targets. This is mind control at its finest, and it occurs when people become brainwashed and molded by the sights and sounds of the world that plays upon their gullibility. Gullibility is described as a failure of social intelligence in which a person is easily tricked or manipulated into an ill-advised course of action. It is closely related to credulity, and this is the tendency to believe unlikely propositions that are unsupported by evidence.

Consider the following historical event:

On October 30, 1938, the world was attacked by Martians! That's right; Martians! This "attack" caused chaos during a fictional radio story by Orson Wells, titled "War of the Worlds". (adapted from the novel by H. G. Wells). In a PBS documentary "American Experience", narrator Oliver Platt says, *"The panic inspired by Welles made "War of the Worlds" perhaps the most notorious event in American broadcast history." An episode of NPR's Radiolab described the effects of the fictional radio program by Wells: "The United States experienced a kind of mass hysteria that we've never seen before."*

The story surrounding this event depicts people in all-out panic due to the belief that the United States was being attacked by alien invaders. It is said that people listening to the broadcast that evening were completely convinced and fearful and that some were arming themselves while attempting to flee into the mountains to escape death. The story says that people were locking their doors and seeking shelter believing that the world was coming to an end. But the reality is that the story about the broadcast was more fictional than the radio broadcast itself!

As the story goes, the story about the effects of the radio broadcast on the public was over exaggerated by the American Experience, program. Their effort was to attract an audience. This was expounded upon in an article written about it. The public was left to juggle a story, about a story, yes, ...about a story, which most likely generated innumerable other stories, which were told by people attempting to explain the um…story!

"Fun Fact: You know who invented the term Fake News? Not Trump. It was Hitler. Look it up. Hitler loved to describe any newspaper that exposed him for what he was as Luegenpresse, which is German for Fake News."

Oliver Markus Malloy, "Inside the Mind of an Introvert"

Kenny Bomer

In an article written by Jefferson Pooley and Michael J. Socolow, about the Orson Wells show, they state:

"The supposed panic was so tiny as to be practically immeasurable on the night of the broadcast. Despite repeated assertions to the contrary in the PBS and NPR programs, almost nobody was fooled by Welles' broadcast."

Yet the more popular story is that the nation was in all-out hysteria! The article goes on to say:

"How did the story of panicked listeners begin? Blame America's newspapers. Radio had siphoned off advertising revenue from print during the Depression, badly damaging the newspaper industry. So, the papers seized the opportunity presented by Welles' program to discredit radio as a source of news. The newspaper industry sensationalized the panic to prove to advertisers, and regulators, that radio management was irresponsible and not to be trusted. In an editorial titled 'Terror by Radio', the New York Times reproached 'radio officials' for approving the interweaving of 'blood-curdling fiction' with news flashes 'offered in exactly the manner that real news would have been given'."

"The nation as a whole continues to face the danger of incomplete, misunderstood news over a medium which has yet to prove ... that it is competent to perform the news job."

("Warned Editor and Publisher," the newspaper industry's Trade Journal)

Does this not sound like the modern-day "War of the Worlds" battle between various news organizations that accuse one another of distributing "fake news"? What are the consumers or innocent, and sometimes not so innocent, bystanders of this ongoing battle, to think or register as truth? Which side are we to trust as we seek to find the truth, while being victims of planned and calculated contrivance? The tricksters of tomfoolery are well acquainted with tactics used in the past, and they have found even more effective ways to mold and shape society without society realizing that it is being manhandled, in this ongoing "War of the Worlds".

"Alternative facts and fake news are just other names for propaganda."

Johnny Corn

6
Media Assassins

"...but no one was interested in the facts. They preferred the invention because this invention expressed and corroborated their hates and fears so perfectly."

James Baldwin, "Notes of a Native Son"

What can sheep do when they come to realize that there is a wolf among them? They must keep the shepherd counting until he becomes aware of the imposter. But by the time the naïve shepherd notices the wolf; many sheep may have already been slaughtered or wounded with their lives being affected in various ways.

The use of the media in influencing people has been discussed in previous chapters, but there is another vital nuance that must not be overlooked as we consider the effect it has on Islam. As with military operations, there are various tactics and strategies utilized to strike the enemy. Some military operations are conducted on a mass scale such as the example of the United States during the final stage of World War II, detonating two nuclear weapons over the Japanese cities of Hiroshima and Nagasaki in August 1945, which killed at least 129,000 to 500,000 people, most of whom were civilians, according to various sources. At the time, former President Truman referenced those bombs as "special bombs", that we now know were atomic bombs, that brought about "special consequences", which calls attention to the concept of "Just War Theory".

In questioning the justification for the killing of innocent people who had nothing to do with actual combat, or the Kamikaze attacks on Pearl Harbor on December 7, 1941, it becomes obvious that people will go to extreme measures to win. The attacks on the two Japanese cities were viewed as "payback" for the attacks on Pearl Harbor. The excuse of trying to end the war by causing the Japanese to surrender was a convenient cover-up for the atrocity. This is a tactic and accompanying excuse that is not accepted in Islam, as the conditions of war were well defined by our Creator in the Holy Qur'an, and the eight rules of engagement explained by Prophet Muhammad (peace be upon him) in the accompanying Hadith (sayings of the Prophet). Those rules of engagement prohibit the killing or destruction of women, children, elderly, non-combatants, religious leaders, animals, religious buildings, trees, and crops.

"God does not prohibit you from showing kindness and being just with those who do not fight you nor have driven you out of your homes. Indeed, God loves those who are just."

Surah Al-Mumtahina 60: 8

The eight rules of engagement in the Hadith can be found on the following website: (https://ilmfeed.com/8-rules-of-engagement-taught-by-the-prophet-muhammad/)

That is Islam! You would never know that if you ignorantly limited yourself to relying upon the hearsay regurgitated from the campaigns of prejudice and hate that are directed against it. Those campaigns have been set in motion by people that will go to any extreme to achieve their goal. As with military campaigns, there are many offensive strategies that are used to gain the upper hand on the enemy. Some of those strategies are obvious, and some are extremely covert.

Some attacks are conducted by using spies or imposters who spew erroneous and incongruous statements as their weapons of choice. They utilize a vast array of tactics and strategies. One of those strategies is *countervalue* – the opposite of counterforce; targeting of enemy cities and civilian populations. Countervalue attacks are used to distract the enemy by drawing focus away from the larger assault. There is no question that the entire Muslim community throughout the world has been targeted using this strategy. This is a strategy that is not limited to combat or military operations. It is a strategy that can be utilized in social, spiritual, and information warfare as well. It is a tactic of influence used to influence the hearts and minds of the target audience for the purpose of mass disruption and persuasion, which affects people mentally, spiritually, socially, and physically at times.

Muslims have been banned, branded, labeled, and attacked mentally, emotionally, spiritually, as well as physically, using this tactic of distraction. This tactic is not new. It has been an ongoing assault on Islam in the media since long before the attacks on 9/11. This tactic has indeed been a distraction for some Muslims who shy away from their faith due to pressures placed on them. Those people succumb to the oppression and attempt to blend in and not be noticed, so they will abandon their faith and practice to go under the radar, distancing themselves from Islam in society. Some will abandon their faith, while others simply attempt to remain low-key due to pressures and fears that have been placed upon them.

Countervalue is an assault on Islam that places Muslims under the pressures of "Anglo conformity". In order to fit into the "melting pot" of Western society, some Muslims will attempt to fit in with the Anglo-Saxon image that has always been presented as being "good". Signs of this can be seen when Muslims begin describing imams as "ministers", the Qur'an as "our Bible", and *masjids* (mosques) as "our Churches" when speaking to non-Muslims.

This type of attack strikes at the heart of the Muslim community and its identity. The most prominent element to this attack is that, despite some Muslims hiding or completely turning away from their faith, the stereotypes and prejudices remain. That realization generates a wide range of emotions in people and causes some to resent being identified as Muslims. That is especially so for people born into Muslim families. These issues, combined with the ease of living a life of self-indulgences, create a cocktail of spiritual and social destruction as the Muslim community gradually implodes from within.

Of course, not all Muslims are affected by the hatred directed towards Islam to a degree that would turn them from it. On the contrary, many Muslims rely even more on faith to overcome the hatred and bigotry that is aimed at Islam. When followed properly, Islam provides a trustworthy handhold that will never break, as mentioned in Surah Al-Baqarah, verse 256, of the Qur'an.

Unlike the hypocrites, the *Mu'min* (true believers) are strengthened by the attacks against Islam and will develop an even stronger reliance upon our Creator as a refuge in dealing with the unprovoked attacks.

On April 16, 1979, *Time* magazine, published an issue that read, "Islam - The Militant Revival" on the cover with a lengthy article "The World of Islam", in which John A. Meyer wrote, "We want to examine Islam's resurgence, not simply as another faith but as a political force and potent third ideology competing with Marxism and Western culture in the world today."

In an article written on the website "The Counter Jihad Report", *by* Ileana Johnson, April 21, 2016, discussing the aforementioned article in *Time* magazine, she states, "No matter how the media spins Islam then and now, Sharia Law and our U.S. Constitution are not compatible. Moral relativism and tolerance to the point of ignorance will result in national suicide."

https://counterjihadreport.com/2016/04/22/a-1979-time-magazine-article-about-islam/

In both articles, Islam and its followers are being undermined by social and mental warfare that is becoming more and more prevalent and extreme. It gives full credence to the saying, "By any means necessary", which is a translation of a phrase used by the French intellectual Jean-Paul Sartre in his play *"Dirty Hands"*, which was popularized by Malcolm X during the Civil Rights Movement.

Another strategy used in warfare is *deception,* which is a strategy that seeks to deceive, trick, or fool the enemy to create a false perception in a way that can be leveraged for a military advantage. The tactic of Deception is just as menacing to Muslims as blatant attacks, and it fits in perfectly with *countervalue* as a one-two punch against Islam.

This represents the "wolf in sheep's clothing" idiom used to describe those playing a role contrary to their real characters. This is enacted by so-called ex-Muslims who not only present themselves as having abandoned Islam but also as having abandoned their belief in God altogether in some instances. Contact with these people is dangerous, particularly because they pose as false teachers, authorities, and experts.

Those individuals are then given a platform by various media sources and presented as "authorities" on Islam. This tactic is a double-edged sword against Islam for the following reasons:

1. Muslims who are weak in faith will use those imposters as an excuse to abandon their own faith. People that are weak and undisciplined in their faith are easily influenced towards taking the easy path of self-indulgences and inclinations. Islam requires obedience to Allah, and that requires effort that must be continuously practiced just like an athlete training for his/her sport. Work and effort are required to achieve success. Unfortunately, most people lack discipline, so many people are led astray by these wolves posing as sheep who are genuinely trying to lead people astray.

"And who does more wrong than the one to whom are recited the Ayat [proofs, evidences, verses, revelations, etc.] of his Lord and then turns away from them? Verily, We shall exact retribution from the Mujrimin [criminals, disbelievers, polytheists, sinners, etc.]."

Surah As-Sajda 32: 22

2. Non-Muslims who don't understand Islam will believe everything that the so-called ex-Muslims say, while totally convinced that those imposters are revealing hidden secrets about Islam that they themselves would not have access to otherwise. They believe whole-heartedly that those imposters have finally come to their senses or have somehow been freed from the snares of Islamic influence. They fail to realize that, in most of these instances, the imposters reveal themselves as frauds through their own words and lack of knowledge or by being exposed when investigated by others. I have debated with myself about whether to mention the fakes and imposters by name or not.

On one hand, I do not want to add to their already existing platform, but, on the other, I want to expose them to draw the reader's attention to this issue. I have chosen to list some of the most well-known imposters while only discussing a few. I encourage the reader to investigate these people instead of focusing on the erroneous and intentionally deceptive claims that they have made.

On the *CNN* program "Anderson Cooper 360°", during a segment titled, "Terror Training Fraud?" the following comment was made:

"Being a counter terrorism expert has been a cottage industry since 9/11. The Department of Homeland Security has spent nearly $40 million on counter terrorism training just since 2006. DHS doesn't keep records on how much is spent just on speakers. But some of the so-called experts who go around the country teaching and, in some cases, preaching about terrorism and the dangers of Islam, are not quite what they seem. People it turns out, like Walid Shoebat."

Drew Griffin, CNN Investigative Reporter

https://www.bing.com/videos/search?q=known+ex+muslim+fakes&&view=detail&mid=668D48AEFFFC1D2A7E98668D48AEFFFC1D2A7E98&&FORM=VDRVRV

Consider the Frauds

Walid Shoebat (claims to be an ex-terrorist turned ultra conservative evangelist)

Dr. Ergun Caner – former Dean of Liberty Baptist University (claims to be a devout ex-Muslim expert on Islam)

Kamal Saleem (claims to be an ex-Muslim terrorist convert to Christianity)

Annis Sharosh (claims to be an ex-Muslim turned Christian evangelist)

Ayaan Hirsi Ali - Dutch feminist and politician (claims to be an ex-Muslim that was mutilated)

Bridget Gabriel – (wrote a book titled *They Must Be Stopped: A Survivor of Islamic Terror*)

Top 5 Christian Evangelists / Fake Ex-Muslims

https://www.youtube.com/watch?v=SiZAto_gNaM

During a live broadcast on CNN in an interview with Ben Shapiro, Bridget Gabriel, a known anti-Muslim Islamophobe made the following comment:

"We must discuss how we can defeat the radicals who want to kill us, who are using the Qur'an as their source and justification for their murders".

Bridgett Gabriel, CNN, with Ben Shapiro

This type of comment is used to mislead the masses into believing that the Qur'an directs Muslims to murder people and that there is something within it that leads people to become "radicalized". This is viewed as being the norm for Muslims by people who simply do not realize that they have been deceived by a person that is profiting large sums of money to make outlandish and unsubstantiated comments against Islam.

Kenny Bomer

It is of no surprise to those that are familiar with these tactics, that people such as Bridgett Gabriel are hand-picked and thrust into the media spotlight as so-called experts on Islam.

Because of her ethnicity, people take what she says as being a valid source of information. They are unaware that it is routine for her, and people like her, to misrepresent the Qur'anic verses about war out of context. Such verses establish rules of engagement always meant for defense of the community and never meant to oppress. It is highly likely that Bridgett Gabriel has no legitimate historical knowledge about those verses of the Qur'an, and most likely doesn't care to. People such as this are paid to be in the spotlight and to disseminate erroneous information as a weapon against Islam while claiming to do it for the sole purpose of administering information.

Brigitte Gabriel also operates under the aliases Hannah Kahwagi Tudor and Brigitte Tudor. She is the CEO, President, and Treasurer of ACT for America. She is a Lebanese-Christian who claims that she came to the United States after surviving the Lebanese civil war. She has made it her mission to warn that radical Muslims, a term she defines as all practicing Muslims, are bent on taking over the West. Before creating ACT, Gabriel was vocally critical of Islam and Muslims. In 2006 she wrote:

"Islamic terrorists ... are really just very devout followers of Muhammad."

The Military Religious Freedom Foundation, a U.S. Veteran's group, refers to Gabriel as "pathologically bigoted".

I propose that people such as Gabriel feel an inner guilt for not being able to adhere to the obligations required for Muslims. It is my belief that the guilt that they feel makes them lash out because they know down deep that they have failed. Instead of correcting themselves and putting forth more effort, they take the easy route and lash out at those that remind them of what they should be doing.

Consider Islam: Disproving the Patriots of Propaganda

Islam is a gift from our Creator. It is a roadmap to success. It is a blueprint for erecting humanity towards righteousness. The only requirement is for people to follow it by putting forth effort necessary to have success. People striving to live righteously in the obedience of Allah influence those close to them, who in turn influence others towards doing what is right and good. God tells us in the Qur'an:

"Let there arise from you a band of people inviting to all that is good, endorsing what is right and forbidding what is wrong. They are the ones to attain felicity."

Surah Al-Imran 3: 104

There is an evil twin to Islamophobia that is just as toxic for society. That twin is *xenophobia,* which is defined as a dislike for people from other countries. In addressing Xenophobia, the late Dr. Jack George Shaheen Jr., a writer and lecturer specializing in addressing racial and ethnic stereotypes. wrote the book, *Reel Bad Arabs*, *The TV Arab,* **and** *Arab and Muslim Stereotyping in American Popular Culture*, undertaking the task of studying 990 movies from the time of silent movies which depicted Arabs and Muslims in a derogatory light. He states, "In all but three of those movies in which Muslims were, "Normalized", all others depicted Arabs or others with ethnic features equated to the stereotypes of Muslims, as "Suicide Bombers", 'rag heads', "belly dancers", and "sand niggers". Those 990 movies represent over a century of slanderous and derogatory stereotypes presented as entertainment to the unconscious minds of the American People.

If people were to sincerely seek the truth, they would realize that Islam has had more of an impact on their lives than they are aware of, be it directly or indirectly, in comprehensive and positive ways. Instead, many engage in what psychologists describe as "confirmation bias", which means that they accept any information that agrees with their worldview or beliefs, while rejecting evidence that is contrary to

79

them. Those people will reject factual evidence in order to stubbornly adhere to their beliefs of choice, despite evidence proving their beliefs to be wrong.

Failure to seek true understanding allows people to lazily rely upon what others have said, which is an easier path for them to take because it requires far less effort to travel that path, while unaware that that path is filled with potholes and detours that do not guide them to the truth. Because they are unaware that they are off course, they just keep on traveling that path, ignoring the signs while relying on verbal commands given by people that are either purposely leading them astray, or who are disastrously lost themselves, who have no true desire to follow the right course because they are so consumed by irrational fear and hatred. They will attempt to suggest that they don't hate, and due to pride will claim fear does not exist, while spreading both continuously through their words and actions. They attack while never being under attack or even threatened themselves.

Allah says in the Qur'an:

"And do not follow that of which you have no knowledge [e.g., one's saying, "I have seen," while in fact he has not seen]. Verily! The hearing, and the sight, and the heart of each of those you will be questioned [by Allah]."

Surah Bani Isra'il 17: 36

7
Why Do They Hate Us?

There is an interesting element to a question like, "Why do they hate us?" It draws to mind additional questions; such as, "Who said they hate you/us?", "Did they tell you they hate you/us?", or "Did someone else tell you those people hate you/us?" The bigger question is, "Who is the "someone" that told you that "they" hate you/us?

The question, "Why do they hate us?", has been a popular slogan used in the media to suggest that Muslims hate non-Muslims, and many non-Muslims have come to believe that even without experiencing any form of hatred for themselves. The fact is, as a Muslim revert of thirty-three years, I can say that I have never ever heard a single Muslim say anything about hating non-Muslims. Nor have I heard Muslims attempting to condemn others to Hell, as I did when I was a Christian and many times since. Being a Caucasian male in the United States, I have witnessed many prejudiced comments by people who had no clue that I am Muslim. Comments of hatred and divisiveness and an "us vs them" attitude from people that will smile in your face and then speak very harshly about you the second you walk away. This is one of the reasons that have driven me to write this book.

Fear is being manufactured in the media and that is obvious. It is an emotion that has been preyed upon since the creation of Man. The great deceiver Satan, or "Iblis" as named in the Qur'an, operated in fear. That fear generated the first sins ever committed –the sins of fear, arrogance, pride, prejudice, bigotry, and hatred. Allah knows best.

When Allah created the Prophet Adam (peace be upon him), Satan was not happy about it. He despised Adam (peace be upon him) because he feared that Adam (peace be upon him) was replacing him as the best of God's creation. Satan was filled with hatred, animosity, prejudice, disdain, jealousy, and envy. He hated Adam (peace be upon him). Satan (Iblis) was the first racist and hate monger. The Qur'an describes Satan as being of the Jinn, spirit-beings made of a smokeless blue flame, whereas Adam (peace be upon him) was created from clay. Like humans, the Jinn have the freedom of choice, unlike the angels who operate like soldiers of our Creator in always following His commands. The Jinn live in the spirit world like the Angels, but they can be persuaded to do good or evil. The Jinn that are led to do evil are the Shaitan (satans or devils). The Shaitan are the evil Jinn that look to influence Man into doing evil. They are led by Iblis, more commonly known as Satan. He is a sworn and avowed enemy to Man. His declaration as a sworn enemy to Man, came about due to "fear" because Satan/Iblis did not want to lose his perceived status.

"And surely, We created you [i.e., your father Adam] and then gave you shape [the noble shape of a human being]; and then, We told the angels, "Prostrate yourselves to Adam," and they prostrated themselves, except Iblîs [Satan]. He refused to be of those who prostrated themselves. (Allâh) said, "What prevented you [O Iblîs] that you did not prostrate yourself, when I commanded you? "Iblîs said, "I am better than him [Adam]. You created me from fire, and You created him from clay." (Allâh) said, "[O Iblîs] get down from this [Paradise]. It is not for you to be arrogant here. Get out, for you are of those humiliated and disgraced." (Iblîs) said, "Allow me respite till the day they are raised up [i.e., the Day of Resurrection]." (Allâh) said, "You are of those respited." (Iblîs) said, "Because You have sent me astray, surely I will sit in wait against them [human beings] on Your Straight Path. Then I will come to them from before them and behind them, from their right and from their left, and You will not find most of them to be grateful." (Allâh) said (to Iblîs) "Get out from this [Paradise] disgraced and expelled. Whoever of them [mankind] will follow you, then surely I will fill Hell with you all."

Qur'an Al Araf 7: 11-18

Satan's influence on Man has been effective in causing division. Because he was removed from Paradise and separated from Allah, he has sought to cause division in mankind through a variety of tactics. He has caused division among mankind, as well as division between Man and our Creator. Yet this whole situation has been allowed by Allah to distinguish those who live obediently from those who choose to do otherwise. Everything is a test. Satan can't force anyone to do anything. He can only whisper suggestions. The choice is yours.

This division among brothers in humanity begins at the top with people of power. Those are the people that have the ability and resources to move masses of people in one direction or another through their own social whisperings. The driving force behind their efforts is fear. Like Satan, they fear losing their positions of "power", and so they make continuous effort to maintain it no matter what the cost. This has been a common theme among people of power and prestige in dealing with commoners in society, in preventing them from rising up in revolt. To prevent this, a common goal is established, often centered on war. War seems to draw people together with a sense of patriotism. During wartime, commoners are used to accomplish specific goals and so they feel like they are part of the team fighting for a so-called just cause. This cause is made out to be approved by God himself, and so people put their hearts into fighting or supporting God and country against an often, not so well-defined enemy. Without the enemy, there is no cause, and so unity is not as strong among commoners and higher powers in periods of peace as it is in times of war. Or so it seems. The enemy must be presented to the common man as an evil threat that must be dealt with. So, the poor and middle class go off to fight wars for the rich minority. They fire guns at people that never wronged them.

Yet they often do so while hating and despising the people they are going to attack. This transpires among soldiers as well as civilians. The people accusing others of hate are trained to be the haters themselves, and they are brainwashed into dehumanizing the alleged enemy.

In order to persuade the common man into believing that the cause is just, carefully crafted slogans are spoken by government leaders and then repeated in the media until the seeds of persuasion begin to grow. Those efforts of persuasion are the very weeds that are choking society at its roots. Those weeds grow in a soil saturated by lies and hidden agendas that are concocted to guarantee that the financially elite remain in power as any and all threats are systematically eliminated. In order for such campaigns to be successful, an enemy must be established with unquestionable surety being emblazoned and ingrained in the minds of the people, which all too often fail to define and depict exactly who the enemy is. We see an example of the slogans used to define who the enemy is in a statement made by former United States President George W. Bush when he said the following:

"Every nation, in every region, now has a decision to make. Either you are with us, or you are with the terrorists."

George W. Bush

A statement such as that allows for no wiggle room in distinguishing who the bad guys are from the good guys. It seems to have been spoken to make people believe that the cause was just by plagiarizing from the Bible, as if God was in support of the endeavor.

"He who is not with me is against me, and he who doesn't gather with me, scatters."

Matthew 12: 30 KJV

People are left with no other option but to conclude that the bad guys are not the United States, but "those people over there" who are labeled as "terrorists". But such a vague statement does not define exactly who the "terrorists" are, and so this forces people to use inductive reasoning to decipher and identify who the bad guys are.

Inductive reasoning uses broad and often flawed, sweeping generalizations in defining and predicting or forecasting potential behaviors. An example would be the following: "Some pit bulls have an overly aggressive and vicious temperament and often attack people and other animals, so they should be euthanized in order to prevent the attacks." Inductive reasoning would imply that "all pit bulls" are by nature prone to attack people, so all of them should be euthanized. Of course, some pit bulls are wonderful and gentle loving pets, but my choice of using that particular breed is indicative of inductive reasoning regarding the stereotypes about pit bulls because many people do believe that they are dangerously over aggressive without having ever been attacked by one or even knowing someone else who was attacked. Pit bulls have been irrationally demonized and branded despite logic and reason which dictates and demands that not all pit bulls are prone to attack people or other animals, despite their obvious ability to do so. The fact is, despite their breed, all dogs have the potential to attack people, but it is the pit bull breeds that are victims of propaganda in society even to the extent that the show "Pit Bulls and Parolees" depicts pit bulls and felons as coming together in order to rehabilitate one another. Like the pit bull, people with a Middle Eastern appearance have been unjustly categorized and associated with terrorism simply due to their appearance, national origin, and/or religious preference. This has occurred due to the broad strokes of overgeneralization that have failed to pin-point exactly who the "terrorists" are.

More examples of slogans that have contributed to this unjustifiable stereotyping are, "We in the civilized world," which implies that no other group of peoples are civilized, which leads people to feel that they are better than others. Another slogan that fails to define the enemy leading to broad generalizations is, "The War on Terror," which is an ambiguous phrase that opens the door to entire groups of people being unjustifiably associated with terrorism.

The final nail in the coffin of condemnation of Muslims was

hammered into the minds of people during the 2016 Presidential Election, when soon-to-be President Donald J. Trump made the following comments during an interview with CNN news anchor, Anderson Cooper. When Cooper asked, "Do you think Islam is at war with the West?" the soon-to-be President Trump stated:

"I think Islam hates us. There is something there. There is a tremendous hatred there. We have to get to the bottom of it. There is an unbelievable hatred of us."

Donald J. Trump

When questioned about this by Anderson Cooper who asked, "Is there a war between the West and radical Islam or is the war between the West and Islam itself?", Trump replied, "Its radical, but it's very hard to define; it's very hard to separate because you don't know who is who."

Trump went on to implement the Muslim-ban only days after being elected President. Trump's comments continue to add fuel to the fires of fear and hatred that are burning at the heart of society, not only in the United States, but throughout the world. Lines have been drawn in the sand and the so-called enemy has been spotlighted as Islam, which has been positioned as a worldwide enemy due to inflammatory and inaccurate comments.

The tactics used to maintain control have been repeated numerous times throughout history, because Man is a creature of habit. Man finds what works, studies it, and then he sticks to it while striving to tweak and make improvements here and there. Note the parallels used in the following two statements which were made over a century apart, but are comprised of similar rhetoric used to push people towards a common goal in facing the designated targets defined in each of those campaigns and considered "Crusades".

In inciting the 1st Crusade on November 27, 1095, Pope Urban II made the following announcement:

"God has conferred upon you, above all nations.... great glory in arms. Undertake this (Crusade), for the remissions of your sins, with the assurance of the impressionable glory
of the kingdom of heaven."

Then on September 16, 2001, former President George W. Bush made the following comment:

"This is a new kind of evil, and we understand, and the American people are beginning to understand. This crusade, this war on terrorism, is going to take a while."

Nearly two decades after the horrific attacks on 9/11, this crusade still being waged against Islam and innocent Muslims who had nothing to do with those attacks. Muslims were killed in those attacks just as others were. Muslims have been killed by terrorists more than any other group of people worldwide! Yet, Islam is still vilified, and hatred has only increased. Despite that, Islam is the fastest growing religion in every country in the world, with most reverts being females. Society has defined Islam as its target, and actions are being taken routinely against it in the hopes to eradicate it; nevertheless, the truth and beauty of Islam continues to grow as more and more people have begun researching the truth.

This is not a new phenomenon or invention, as we have seen this occur many times in history. A prime example of this is the annihilation of the Native Americans in the United States. They were slaughtered by the millions, and then their history was written for them by the ancestors of their oppressors. They have been presented as savages in the history books, movies, and on television, etc., for the most part; whereas, the Caucasian settlers from Europe have been presented as the "Founding Fathers".

When people dig deep into the history of Native Americans, it becomes obvious that great atrocities have been enacted against them and that the history books have been hiding things that tarnish the image of the "settlers". They could easily be described as "immigrants", a term conveniently pushed to the side when referencing those people. The fact is, the Native Americans were raped, pillaged, and slaughtered by the millions. Their land and resources were stolen from them by white Europeans who then gathered the original citizens together on "reservations" as if to make amends for the atrocities.

"History is always written by the winners. When two cultures clash, the loser is obliterated, and the winner writes the history books-books which glorify their own cause and disparage the conquered foe. As Napoleon once said, 'What is history, but a fable agreed upon?'"

Dan Brown, The Da Vinci Code

I am not suggesting that the issues regarding anti-Islam and Islamophobic campaigns of hate are equivalent to or more significant than the atrocities committed against the Native Americans or any other group that has been targeted throughout history, and I by no means wish to undermine t those events. Nor am I suggesting that these issues of prejudice and racism are limited to the United States. Obviously, this has been a worldwide campaign of hate which has been propagated and driven by fear, as history again repeats itself with another group being singled out in the world. In a statement submitted by his campaign during his bid for the Presidency, in 2016, Senator Ted Cruz, the United States representative for my home state of Texas made the following comments:

"Our European allies are now seeing what comes of a toxic mix of migrants who have been infiltrated by terrorists and isolated, in radical Muslim neighborhoods."

"We need to empower law enforcement to patrol and secure Muslim neighborhoods before they become radicalized."

International Business Times

If you tie all of this together with the previous quotes from former President George W. Bush, who was calling all nations to come together against Islam, it is not surprising that the United States could be successful in persuading other countries to band together against Islam.

In an article written by U.K. writer, Peter Oborne, published in the *Daily Mail* newspaper (July 4, 2008) he stated the following:

"Islamophobia - prejudice against Islam - is Britain's last remaining socially respectable form of bigotry, and we should be ashamed of ourselves for it. This dangerous demonizing of the country's 1.6 million Muslim inhabitants is happening all around us."

Peter Oborne

This hatred for Islam, which is being fueled by Islamophobic rhetoric and propaganda, is nothing new. It has existed since the days of Prophet Muhammad (peace be upon him). He and his companions were hated and despised by the people of Mecca, who attacked the Muslims in a variety of ways. The Muslims were slandered, physically assaulted, killed, and were driven out of their homes after sanctions were implemented against them by their Meccan neighbors. The Muslims had no choice but to leave Mecca for a period of eight years, during which Islam grew from being comprised of a mere handful of followers to ten thousand in number. At that point, the Muslims returned to reclaim Mecca peacefully, not killing a single one of those who oppressed them. When questioned by his followers about what to do about those who oppressed them just a few years prior, Prophet Muhammad (peace be upon him) instructed the Muslims not to harm them and to allow them their religious freedom. The Prophet (peace be upon him) did destroy the three hundred and sixty false idols that were surrounding the Kaaba, and, by doing so, the Muslims reclaimed the House of our Creator. Muslims have been in control of Mecca ever since.

Despite efforts to stop Islam from expanding, Islam grew rapidly in the days of Prophet Muhammad (peace be upon him), and we see rapid growth in current times. The hatred of those hypocrites that attempt to suggest that Muslims are being inspired to hate by Islam, have had their effort backfire on them time and time again. The curiosity that they are invoking through their relentless efforts have caused many to follow them in their divisive campaigns, but it has also inspired many people to sincerely investigate the fallacious claims made against Islam.

When people are willing to set aside preconceived notions and pre-suppositions in order to seek the truth for themselves, they will see that Islam is far from being the evil religion that they have been led to believe it is. They will come to realize that the Islamophobic hate mongers have denied what Islam truly is while spreading lies and misconceptions about what it is not.

8
Where the Enemy Lies

Islam is a complete and comprehensive means to acquire peace by submitting to Allah. Islam is perfect. It is an avenue for success in this life and the hereafter. While Islam is perfect, people are not, and so Islam has been mishandled and misunderstood by people who truly believe their interpretation and understandings about Islam are correct. Additionally, there are those who spread lies claiming that Islam is something that it is not, while denying what it is.

These varying beliefs have existed since early Islam, which were generated by various levels of intellect, lack of knowledge, cultural persuasions, traditions, political ambitions, man's desire for power, and inclinations towards evil. All of which has been preyed upon by Islamophobes and terrorists who have hijacked Islam in order to achieve their agendas. Both of those groups have led people astray due to their own radical views of Islam that do not represent the beliefs held by the vast majority of Muslims in the world living in peace and harmony while having an entirely different views of Islam. Views which are based on the totality of Islamic teachings, unlike the views held by Islamophobes and Terrorists who resort to cherry-picking verses of the Qur'an in order to achieve their evil agendas and political goals. The true believer considers the entirety of guidance in Islam, which is always consistent.

That consistency leads to sincerity of faith in the believer's heart. The true believers surrender to being rightly guided by the speech of Allah in the Qur'an, as well as the Sunnah (example) of Muhammad (peace be upon him) as an example of guidance in everyday life. But sometimes that guidance is misinterpreted or misunderstood, leading to controversy and contention among followers who possess various levels of intellect and knowledge and, therefore, beliefs.

Due to varying levels of intellect and beliefs, Islam seen division taking place within a quarter century after the death of Prophet Muhammad (peace be upon him), as the Muslims sought to choose a proper successor to lead them. That division resulted in the advent of Sunni and Shia Islam.

Over time there developed five traditions in Islam that contested with one another. Each group held different interpretations about certain fundamental beliefs of Islam and its message. The Mutazilites stressed reason and logic. The Murjites believed peace was incumbent upon all Muslims and that political leadership was not worth engaging in war and that all Muslims are equal. Followers of Sunni Islam are the "legalists" who believe that Sharia should be implemented into Islam. Sufism represents mystics who believe that they can obtain oneness with Allah through inner life moral purification. The fifth division was the Kharijites who represent those with radical extremist views.

The Kharijites considered anyone that believed differently from them to be Kafur (unbelievers). They also believed that one who commits major sin is a Kafir and no longer a Muslim. They believe those people could be killed, and their wealth could be divided among the Muslims. They believed that those people would be in Hell forever. They justified their beliefs by stating, "You agree with us that deeds are a part of faith, because faith is composed of belief, words, and deeds. If one part of faith, such as actions, is missing, then the whole of faith is absent."

The Kharijites were true fanatics and radicals in the same way that ISIS is in modern times. They represent a violent and politicized version of Islam. They do not hesitate in massacring people who they believe are not obeying Islam exactly the way they understand Islam to be. They take no issue with killing both Muslims and non-Muslims as they seek to destroy adversaries and/or competing versions of Islam that exist. It was people with this mentality that killed Ali, the fourth

Caliph of Islam, because they believed that Abu Bakr was the rightful successor to lead the Muslims after the death of Prophet Muhammad (peace be upon him), and it is people with this similar mentality that will killanyone today that they deem to be Kafurs (nonbelievers), who don't agree with them.

In an article written on October 12, 2001, by David F. Forte titled "Understanding Islam and the Radicals", he stated:

"Osama bin Laden is making war on Islam the way Joseph Stalin made war on Russia, the way Mao Zedong made war on China. It is in this sense that the radicals have hijacked traditional Islam and are the Marxist vanguard of a new Islam, to be imposed on the rest of the Muslim society--and the rest of the world. If bin Laden has his way, the Taliban would be the Islam for all Muslims. It would usher in a dark age that that great civilization has not seen the equal of."

The acts committed by terrorists are un-Islamic and so they can be deemed as unbelievers. They kill more Muslims worldwide than any other group of people. That fact places them in the category of "non-believers" in rejecting the fundamentals of true Islam. As previously mentioned, Islam prohibits the killing of women, children, elderly people, religious leaders, non-combatants, and civilians –all of whom died during the horrific attacks on 9/11.

Islam mandates that if Islam itself is not directly under attack, and if Islam can be freely practiced, war is not permitted. Yet the radicals have no problem in violating the fundamental teachings of Islam in order to achieve their political goals. This means that anyone and everyone that is in opposition to their beliefs is seen as the enemy. This is especially true for true believers that speak out against them. Muslims throughout the world continue to speak out against acts of terror, but the efforts are overshadowed by misinformation spread by the two sects of radicals that exist in the world today. The Islamophobes and the terrorists spread horrendous lies and misconceptions about Islam on a routine basis.

Each of those two groups have affected Muslims in very damaging ways. They have caused doubt and disbelief to exist in the minds of some Muslims who are less knowledgeable and therefore easily impressionable. Those unlearned Muslims will sometimes join the ranks of the radicals because they fail to correctly comprehend verses of the Qur'an that address war in its proper context. They may abandon their faith altogether, due to the pressures of Islamophobia, or because they begin to believe that Islam is the evil and intolerant religion that the Islamophobes and terrorists have made it out to be.

Non-Muslims have also been affected in a variety of ways by the radical Islamophobes and terrorists. They often develop a great hatred and disdain for Islam because they believe that the picture of Islam that has been presented to them in the media represents true Islam. They are not aware that the true beauty of Islam has been smudged time and time again, by the radicals that paint pictures of Islam that do not represent it correctly. Those images have been painted with broad, ugly strokes of death, lies, and deceptions that have been presented as the norm for Islam despite the overwhelming number of peaceful Muslims in the world.

Islam continues to spread despite the efforts of the radicals whether they are Islamophobes who fear that Muslims are planning to take over the world and implement Sharia and the terrorists who do not follow the true path of Allah as believers in peace and equality for all of mankind.

By the Will of Allah, more and more people are being exposed to Islam, and as they investigate and do research, many are beginning to realize that the canvasses of Islam that have been presented to them have been darkened by lies and deceptions, and many are beginning to accept and embrace Islam. People are starting to realize that Islam is not the evil religion that the radicals have made it out to be. They are beginning to recognize the lies and deceptions of the radicals and Islamophobes, residing on both sides of the fence, as Islam stands in the middle ground proving what it is and what it is not.

It is the obligation of true believers to be good ambassadors of Islam and to represent it through righteous actions and deeds so that the true beauty of Islam is revealed through the Ummah (faith community) of Muhammad (peace be upon him) one person at a time and collectively. The true believers seek knowledge and understanding, and, by doing so, protect themselves and the rest of society from being misled by those that prove themselves to be unbelievers.

Through their un-Islamic actions and beliefs, the extremists distinguish themselves from true believers, setting themselves apart from true Islam. They prove themselves to be believers of falsehood and proponents of evil, who are bent on achieving their goals.

"Instead [of playing sport], We hurl truth against deceit in order to destroy (deceit), and then deception perishes. Beware of incurring misery because of your [false] descriptions [of God]."
Surah Al-Anbiyah 21: 18

The consistency of a man defines who he is. The consistency of believers as compared to radicals differentiates the rightly guided from those who have attempted to redefine the truth, proving themselves to be misled. The path of Allah is a straight path that is well defined, and traveling it requires guidance that leads humanity to good while bypassing the pitfalls of evil. Comparing true believers with extremists is like comparing night to day.

"Allah disdains not to use the similitude of things lowest as well as highest. Those who believe know that it is truth from their Lord, but those who reject Faith say, 'What does Allah mean by this similitude?' By it He causes many to stray, and He leads many into the right path, but He causes not to stray, except those who forsake [the path]. Those who break Allah's Covenant after it is ratified and who break apart

95

what Allah has ordered to be joined and do evil on earth cause loss [only] to themselves."

Surah Al-Baqarah 2: 26-27

Islam guides humanity to equality and justice and tolerance for those of other religions, races, and nationalities. Those who think otherwise simply don't know the truth, don't care to know the truth, have purposely distorted the truth, or have accepted the words of the antagonists as being truth instead of discussing these issues with Muslims, or in lieu of relying upon Muslim sources for their information. Therefore, we see non-Muslims and radicals attempting to define and explain what Muslims think and believe, even to the extent that at times they have the audacity to tell Muslims what Muslims themselves believe! This is a very common occurrence, but unless you are a Muslim experiencing this ludicrous situation first-hand on a routine basis, you will not understand how problematic and absurd this is for Muslims who face this constantly.

The issues on the other side of the fence are just as pressing as the Islamic extremists attempt to redefine Islam. Their intention is to reform the minds of Muslims from tolerance to extremism, and so moderate Muslims are stuck in the middle of an all-out assault on Islam from various fronts. True, peaceful Muslims have propagators of fear on one side, with the frightened and fearful on the other directing the blame at the fundamentals of Islam, as some people in the world believe that moderate Muslims are just an "Allah Akbar" away from becoming terrorists.

One of the most difficult things for Muslims to cope with in dealing with these campaigns of fear is the fact that some Muslims who are not very knowledgeable about Islam are somewhat impressionable and easily misguided, and so we see some younger or unlearned Muslims abandoning Islam or resorting to extreme views. Some will leave Islam for another religion, but many abandon their religion altogether, becoming atheists. This happens because of the constant mislabeling and misconceptions about Islam that are promoted by people who have not taken time to do study and research and by the hi-jackers of faith who distort the truth. Therefore, Muslims are required to continuously seek knowledge about Islam. The more one engages in study, the stronger one's faith becomes, and so seeking knowledge is the best way to combat the lies that are perpetuated against Islam.

Knowledge gives one the tools necessary to correct lies and misconceptions told by those who seem obsessed with trying to suggest that Islam is an evil and false religion. We are obligated as Muslims to seek knowledge and to share it. Sharing it is a defense done verbally and in deeds.

The beauty and truth of Islam is best demonstrated through the words and actions of the individual, as well as the worldwide body of Muslims as a whole. Muslims are guided to be hospitable, patient, caring, charitable, and to avoid any form of oppression towards another. So, this means that when dealing with those who ridicule and attack Islam, we as Muslims should counter hateful rhetoric by being patient, and never being discouraged in our efforts while dealing with the hatred and ignorance of those who seek to cause division. Our Creator (Allah) tells us exactly how to deal with those people who spread hatred and prejudice by mentioning them in the Qur'an in several places.

"And not equal are the good deed and the bad. Repel [evil] by that [deed] which is better; and then, you may make an intimate friend of one with whom there was hatred."
Surah Fussilat 41: 34

"Invite to the way of your Lord with wisdom and good instruction and argue with them in a way that is best. Indeed, your Lord is most knowing of who has strayed from His way, and He is most knowing of who is rightly guided."
Surah An-Nahl 16: 125

97

The greatest enemy of Islam, other than Shaitan (Iblis the Satan), is ignorance. The greatest weapon to combat ignorance is knowledge. Knowledge is a weapon that disrupts ignorance at its core, and it is knowledge that gives mankind the ability to fight off Shaitan himself! Therefore, Allah tells mankind to seek knowledge and to ponder, think, and reflect on creation, science, as well as the history of former peoples.

The very first commandment from our Creator in the Qur'an is:

"Proclaim! [or Read!] in the name of thy Lord and Cherisher, Who created –Created Man from a [mere] clot of congealed blood. Proclaim! And thy Lord is Most Bountiful --He Who taught [the use of] the Pen — Taught man that which he knew not. Nay, but man transgresses all bounds, In that he looks upon himself as self-sufficient. Verily, to your Lord is the return [of all]."

Surah Al-Alaq 96: 1-8

In order to combat ignorance, lies, deceptions, and misconceptions, it is important that people seek knowledge. Knowledge provides the Muslims the tools necessary to respond to false accusations in the best of manners and it provides the non-Muslim with a proper understanding of Islam, which brings about attitudes of tolerance and acceptance in society.

People are easily influenced by soundbites or news segments of thirty-five seconds or less, and they feel that they have been well informed. But true understanding requires time and effort that most people have no interest in sacrificing. People are busy with life and dealing with various tests and trials, and seeking knowledge is often pushed to the back burner. The burden resides on those that do have a genuine interest and concern for seeking the truth, in sharing what they know with others.

There is no time to waste! Wasted time is wasted opportunity, and this affects each one of us in society. Time is like ice melting away, so it is important for us as human beings to use time to seek wisdom, knowledge, and understanding in an effort to melt away the ignorance, lies, and deceptions that have made the hearts of many people cold and dark.

Allah warns us about the use of time in the Qur'an by stating:

"By [the token of time [through the Ages, Verily Man is in loss, Except for those who have faith and do righteous deeds and unite in the mutual teaching of truth, patience, and constancy."

Surah Al-Asr 103: 1-3

CONSIDER THE TIME!

CONSIDER ISLAM!

9
Momma Mia No Sharia!

I named this chapter after an internet radio program on Patriot Radio that goes by this ridiculous name. There are about six shows on Patriot Radio that attack Islam daily or weekly. I have engaged one of the talk show hosts in debate in the past at the request of a Muslim sister that wanted me to respond to that man's ignorant claims. He and people like him routinely discuss Islam as if they have a sure knowledge about what they are discussing, while in fact they do not. They are leading many people astray through their ignorance and hate-filled rhetoric. Sharia is one of the issues that they address most.

Despite growing numbers, many people throughout the world detest, hate, despise, loath, and are completely obsessed and consumed by an irrational fear in thinking that Muslims are planning to take over the world like some extraterrestrial beings in a science fiction movie out to implement Sharia law. Most of those people have no clue as to what Sharia law is, but are terrified in believing Muslims are plotting and planning to implement it. The fact is, most Muslims themselves don't know exactly what Sharia is in all its dynamics. Sharia is simply commandments from God to humanity. Within the commandments are accompanying consequences for good and bad deeds. It is a matter of cause and effect. For every action there is a reaction, and the outcome of any given action will bring about a just consequence or reward. When mankind does good, the reward is pleasing to Man. When mankind commits acts of evil, difficulties arise. These actions and accompanying reactions affect the individual as well as anyone else in society that may be affected by good or bad decisions or actions of the individual. Sharia is a means to regulate, compensate, or penalize mankind based on the Wisdom of our Creator.

"Verily, proofs have come to you from your Lord, so whoever sees will do so for [the good of] his own self, and whoever blinds himself, will do so to his own harm, and I [Muhammad] am not a watcher over you."

Surah al-Anaam 6: 10

Much of the fear about Islam and Sharia has been propagated by people who hypocritically accuse Islam of spreading hate and subjugation, while hating and subjugating people themselves. This is not to imply that there are no Muslims in the world with hatred in their hearts; to make such a claim would be nonsensical and unrealistic. What I am saying is that Islam does not promote hatred or oppression of others despite popular belief. Note the following comments made in the Hadith of Prophet Muhammad (peace be upon him) during his last sermon before his death.

"O People, listen to me in earnest, worship God [The One Creator of the Universe], perform your five daily prayers (Salah), fast during the month of Ramadan, and give your financial obligation (zakat) of your wealth. Perform Hajj if you can afford to. All mankind is from Adam and Eve. An Arab has no superiority over a non-Arab, and a non-Arab has no superiority over an Arab; also, a white has no superiority over a black, and a black has no superiority over white except by piety and good deeds."

(Delivered on the Ninth day of Dhul al Hijjah, 10 A.H., in the 'Uranah valley of Mount Arafat, 632 A.C.)

The definition of Sharia in the Arabic language means, "the path" or "a road that leads to water". Sharia is a set of moral and social guidelines or laws established by our Creator. As our designer, Allah knows that we are prone to do both good and evil, so He tests us in a variety of ways in order to draw our attention to Him. Note what the Qur'an says about being tested by Allah:

"Be sure We shall test you with something of fear and hunger, some loss in goods, lives and the fruits [of your toil], but give glad tidings to those who patiently persevere. Who say, when afflicted with calamity, "To Allah we belong, and to Him is our return." They are those on whom (descend) blessings from their Lord and Mercy, and they are the ones that receive guidance. "

Surah al-Baqarah 2: 155-157

In the process of being guided, we are reminded to stay on the Straight Path of Allah numerous times in the Qur'an, and we ask Allah to help us navigate His Straight Path in every prayer that we recite numerous times daily. It is through patience, prayer, and complete reliance on God in all matters that allow one to navigate His Straight Path successfully. Sharia is the system of rules and guidelines that help make it possible. Note the first chapter of the Qur'an, Surah al-Fatihah (The Opening), which is also the foundation of the Muslim prayer and is similar to the "Our Father" prayer that Jesus (peace be upon him) is said to have taught his disciples in the Bible.

Surah Al-Fatihah (1st Chapter of Qur'an 1: 1-7)

In the name of Allah, the Beneficent, the Merciful.
Praise be to Allah, the Cherisher and Sustainer of the Worlds,
Most Gracious, Most Merciful,
Master of the Day of Judgment.
You do we worship, and Your aid we seek.
Show us the Straight Way.
The way of those on whom You have bestowed Your Grace,
Those whose (portion) is not wrath and who go not astray.

The fact is, Sharia is the commandments from God, that help mankind navigate this life successfully, but the Islamophobes attempt to make it out to be some barbaric inhuman, 6th-century system of oppression. That could not be any further from the truth.

Kenny Bomer

"Sharia represents how practicing Muslims can best lead their daily lives in accordance with God's divine guidance."
Teaching Tolerance, a project of the Southern Poverty Law Center

An example of this divine guidance for humanity is the Ten Commandments of the Bible listed in the *Book of Exodus 20: 1-17*, as well as *Surah Al-Isra 17: 23-39* of the Qur'an. I encourage the reader to read both references and then ask yourself if you agree with these commands or directives? If you agree with them, then you would agree with the concept of Sharia.

Obviously, mankind falls short of living up to and following our Creator's instructions properly. As previously mentioned, most Muslims do not know all the details surrounding Sharia because, though it is a system of guidelines, it is not implemented and followed properly, just as people fail to follow the Ten Commandments of the Bible properly.

"Shariah law, according to Muslims, includes 'the principle of treating other people justly, of making sure that the financial system treats people fairly ... and most importantly the basic principles of Islamic fate'."
Harvard Law Professor Noah Feldman

Of course, most people are concerned about the punishments mentioned in Islamic sources for breaking such commandments, but if they were to investigate the requirements for such punishments, they would realize that there are rules regulating the stipulations for punishments that are nearly impossible to achieve. If more people were aware of that reality, there would be far less fear of the ominous "SHARIA" in the world.

In my mind I could hear a menacing musical score (DUNT DUNT DUNT DUUUUUN) from a Hollywood movie as I typed the word, which may seem silly, but the views regarding Sharia in the world are equivalent to one who has been frightened by something seen on a movie screen, while never being in any real danger at all! Why be injudiciously afraid of something that has not threatened or affected you?

The following quote by media personality Newt Gingrich is just one of many that have people totally convinced that the picture of Islam that is being presented by non-Muslims is accurate, while ignoring the actions of their Muslim neighbors they encounter daily in their communities! Those Muslims are doctors, teachers, professors, lawyers, business owners, etc. who are simply trying to live life like they are. Meanwhile, people such as Gingrich routinely lie about what Islam isn't, while denying what it is.

"Let me be as blunt and direct as I can be. Western civilization is in a war. We should frankly test every person here who is of a Muslim background, and if they believe in sharia, they should be deported. Sharia is incompatible with Western civilization. Modern Muslims who have given up Sharia—glad to have them as citizens. Perfectly happy to have them next door."

Newt Gingrich (on Fox News)

An example of this is the farcical belief of people who seem to be convinced of the threat of being stoned to death by people who aren't holding stones! Let's reflect on one example of a common misconception that demonstrates this. This is one of the many gross misconceptions about Sharia law that has been used to paint an ugly picture of Islam by its enemies. Enemies who seem to have perfected the art of spreading lies about Islam, while making themselves out to be authorities.

Kenny Bomer

Punishment for adultery by stoning under Sharia Law; note the following requirements:

- Stoning for Adultery must be a law of the land in the country in which the adulterous act occurred. If there is no law stipulating this form of punishment, Islam says it can't be done!
- The judgment and verdict must be rendered in a court of law. People have the right to a fair trial and are given the opportunity to defend themselves.
- The accuser must produce three other witnesses. Every witness must have seen actual penetration occur. Accusers cannot be presumptuous in their accusations, meaning they can't say that they saw two people holding hands, hugging, kissing, or spending time together, and claim that the two have committed the (sexual) act of adultery.
- If the accuser does not produce three other witnesses, then they themselves are to be punished for slander against the accused. Each of the witnesses must be known for being
- truthful with no known history of deception by anyone. This means that they must have   never been accused of any form of dishonesty by anyone in their lives.
- Forgiveness is always an option and is preferred. Anytime some type of punishment is mentioned by our Creator in the Qur'an, it is always followed by a verse which says, "But Allah is the Oft-returning, Most Merciful", or something similar.

Let's be honest. Adultery is a horrendous act that affects not only the people committing the act, but their families and society as a whole. Society would be far better off if people were so afraid of the punishment that they would avoid this grave sin. But on the contrary, people selfishly risk the consequences of the act for a few moments of pleasure, while oblivious to those that may be potentially affected by their crime against humanity. Are the adulterers not stoning society through their actions?

Now let's compare those stipulations for punishment, with an example from the Bible and the Qur'an. Note the following Biblical verse, which leads mankind to reflect on the story of Moses (Musa) (peace be upon him) as he dealt with the rebellion of the Children of Israel in the worship of the calf, even after the "Greatest of Commandments" was given.

"Hear, O Israel: The LORD our God, the LORD is one."
Deuteronomy 6: 4 NIV

Then:

"Fear the Lord your God, serve him only and take your oaths in his name. Do not follow other gods, the gods of the peoples around you; for the Lord your God, who is among you, is a jealous God and his anger will burn against you, and he will destroy you from the face of the land."
Deuteronomy 6: 13 NIV

Despite being warned repeatedly, the Children of Israel continued their disobedience, wandering in the desert for what the Bible describes as being forty years. The Bible describes the Prophet Moses (peace be upon him) as being extremely angry and says that God instructed that those in disobedience to Him be killed.

Then he said to them, "This is what the Lord, the God of Israel, says: 'Each man strap a sword to his side. Go back and forth through the camp from one end to the other, each killing his brother and friend and neighbor.'" The Levites did as Moses commanded, and that day about three thousand of the people died."
Exodus 32: 27-28

107

Compare to the same story in the Qur'an:

"And (remember) when Mûsa /Moses) said to his people, 'O my people! Verily, you have wronged yourselves by worshiping the calf. So, turn in repentance to your Creator, and kill yourselves [i.e., the innocent kill the wrongdoers among you]. That will be better for you with your Creator.' Then He accepted your repentance. Truly, He is the One Who accepts repentance, the Most Merciful."

Surat Al-Baqarah 2: 51-54

In the Qur'an, the people repented, and it was accepted from them, so death for punishment for their sin was no longer a requirement because Our Creator is, as I previously mentioned, is At-Tawab (Oft-returning) and Ar-Raman (The Most Merciful). So, the option to forgive is always preferred in Sharia.

Of the thirteen predominantly Muslim countries that follow Sharia, none follow it correctly in all aspects as regulated by Islamic jurisprudence. A variety of factors come in to play regarding interpretations, implementation, and enforcement. The fact is, the term *Sharia* is a term in the Arabic language which means 'a body of moral and religious laws derived from religious prophecy', as opposed to human legislation, which is often flawed. Mankind simply fails to follow it properly. But despite man's failure, Sharia as intended would lead to utopia.

Even so, the fact is that Muslims are not trying to force Sharia on anyone while unable to properly follow it themselves. To think otherwise is an absurdity manufactured solely in the media which leads people to think that way, while incapable of producing evidence to support such irrational claims.

All the while, people are failing to consider the number of Muslims they are likely to encounter in their communities daily. Muslims are your neighbors, public officials, teachers, doctors, public servants, politicians, etc. So, the obvious question is, why fear common everyday people that, like you and I, are just going about their lives trying to be productive and happy members of society while providing for their families? Is it reasonable to think that common everyday people can overthrow the government, creating a new system of law? The fear of change or loss is so great that people become defensive and uncomfortable when presented with circumstances that lie outside of the boundaries of their perceived comfort zones.

People are simply afraid that their lives are going to be altered or disrupted, and so, to cling to their way of life, many will reject anything that is different or foreign to them. So, in this we have the combined effects of xenophobia (i.e., dislike of or prejudice against people from other countries) influencing Islamophobia and vice versa, in a snowball effect that never ceases to grow.

God says in the Qur'an:

"If Allah had so willed, He would have made you a single people, but (His plan is) to test you in what He has given you, so strive as in a race in all virtues. The goal of you all is to Allah; it is He that will show you the truth of the matters in which you dispute."

Surat Al-Maida 5: 43

The preceding verse demonstrates that our Creator has made us of different races and placed us in various parts of the earth for a purpose, and He has gifted peoples of varying ethnicities with certain knowledge and gifts specific to them, which are meant to be shared with other peoples in other areas of the world so that we all benefit from the unique knowledge and cultures that each group of people possess. We see these unique gifts when we travel and are exposed to varying foods, clothing apparels, inventions, resources, etc., as well as arts, sciences, discoveries, and, yes, religions. We see this same diversity within our local communities as we dine and experience various types of food and cultures while interacting with people of other races and nationalities, yet when one group is targeted and unjustifiably labeled in campaigns against them, we see hatred and rejection of that group and a gross intolerance for them abroad as all sense of reason is systematically dissolved by continuous propaganda and poisonous, hate-filled rhetoric which has been injected into the veins of society like poison.

Islam is the anecdote for that poison. Islam demands that the laws of the land in which Muslims reside be followed and that respect be given to those of authority if the laws do not adversely affect the fundamental rules of Islam. If Muslims are not forced to commit crimes or sin against our Creator's commandments and as long as religious freedom is given, observing the laws of society in the land is following Sharia!

10
Christians and Atheists

I have engaged many stubborn and unnecessarily rude people while doing *Dawah* (witnessing) and defending Islam. I always strive to avoid making comments that are offensive Muslims are obligated to live by a higher standard. Nevertheless, I have at times found myself extremely angry because of the constant bombardment of derogatory comments that are made by atheists as well as Christians! Christians and atheists routinely side with one another in mutual hatred and dislike for Islam. This is a very shocking thing to experience. It is in those times of anger and shock that Muslims are instructed to be patient because these issues have existed throughout history. Every prophet (peace be upon them all) experienced far worse atrocities than we ever will. So, no matter what is said, Muslims should remain patient and calm and implore wisdom.

Allah tells us in the Qur'an:

"Invite (all) to the way of thy Lord with wisdom and beautiful preaching; and argue with them in ways that are best and most gracious: for thy Lord knoweth, best who have strayed from His Path, and who receive guidance."

Surat An-Anal 16:124

Modern technology has allowed hate mongers to have a voice that they might not otherwise have. Social media provides the opportunity for those people to spread their lies and misconceptions about Islam to anyone that will listen, and listen they do. There are large numbers of internet talk/radio shows, as well as social media groups, that do nothing but paint an ugly picture of Islam on a weekly or even a daily basis. Some shows are hosted by atheists, and some by Christians. Some of those shows are produced by individuals, and some are produced by groups of people that make it a point to discuss Islam routinely. Many of the people that host the shows utilize fake names in order to remain anonymous and will often claim to be ex-Muslims. These people present themselves as authorities on Islam, and their naïve followers believe they are! But anyone who has even a basic knowledge about Islam can tell that most of those people have no clue at all about what it is they are discussing.

I am purposely avoiding mentioning any of those individuals or their programs because I do not want to help elevate their platform. I am simply trying to make the reader aware that this method of attack in discrediting and misconstruing Islam exists, and people should verify from whom they are getting information. Some of those people even go to the extremes of taking time out to create fake social media accounts pretending to be Muslim in order to make Muslims look bad. This is a tactic used by Christians and atheists alike. I have experienced this myself personally.

Consider how much hatred and disdain there must be in one's heart that would lead them to take time out of their lives on a routine basis in order to attack Islam. Seldom do the Christian hosts of those shows discuss Christianity, and the atheists spend countless hours attacking a God, Prophet (peace be upon him), and religion, while not believing any of it is real! Many people disbelieve in the existence of unicorns, but shows are not being produced to discuss and spread lies about unicorns! Why? Because people have not been trained to hate unicorns like they have been trained to hate Islam.

The positive impact that Islam has had on society in the fields of medicine, technology, mathematics, chemistry, physics, urbanization, art, poetry, politics, social justice, and detailed codes of conduct regarding etiquette and respect for all people is evident by the actions of the overwhelming number of followers of Islam, that contribute as productive members of society. Yet it appears that doing positive things isn't news worthy in society, which seems to be more interested in and entertained by violence, sexual exploits, intoxicants, rumors, and gossip than it is in hearing stories about people standing against all those things based on the teachings of their religion. Islam provides the solution for all of those negative issues in society, which is demonstrated by the way the common, everyday Muslim man and woman conduct themselves. For example, based on research conducted by the Pew Research Center, Muslims have lower divorce, alcohol, drug use, domestic violence, child abuse, abortion, sexual immorality, suicide, and murder rates than any other major religion.

Note the following verses of the Qur'an and Hadith regarding those topics:

Alcohol and other intoxicants are forbidden in Surah Al-Ma'ida 5: 90-1.

Suicide is condemned in Sahih al-Bukhari 71: 670 and 73: 73.

Abortion is not allowed based on Hadith in Sahih al-Bukhari 54: 430 which says that a fetus has a soul within 120 days of gestation. Islam not only prohibits female infanticide, but it also forbids all types of infanticide, irrespective of whether the infant is a male or female. It is mentioned in Surah Al-Anaam 6: 151:

"Do not kill your children on a plea of want. We provide sustenance for you and for them. Do not come near shameful deeds, whether open or secret. Do not take life which Allah has made sacred."

A similar guidance is repeated in Surah Al-Isra 17: 31:

"Do not kill your children for fear of want. We shall provide sustenance for them as well as for you. Verily, the killing of them is a great sin."

Kenny Bomer

Sex outside of marriage is forbidden by Surah Al-Isra17: 32 and Surah An-Noor 24: 2-5.

A Hadith in Sahih al-Bukhari 34: 439 forbids prostitution.

Certain verses of the Quran indicate that homosexual activity is forbidden: (Surah Ash-Shu-ara 26: 165-66 and Surah Al-A'raf 7: 80-4).

Surah At-Tahrim 65 specifies certain conditions under which divorce is permissible.

The Qur'an and Hadith do not condone honor killings; that is, taking the life of a family member who has allegedly brought shame on his or her family. See Gill, Aisha, 2011, "Reconfiguring 'Honor'-Based Violence as a Form of Gendered Violence." In Idriss, Mohammad Mazher and Tahir Abbas, editors, *Honor, Violence, Women and Islam;* Routledge, pages 222-223.

Many people are unaware that the Qur'an and authentic Hadith (sayings of the Prophet Muhammad (peace be upon him) address any and everything that we human beings will ever experience in life. Islam is a complete and comprehensive set of guidelines that will guide mankind to success in all areas if those guidelines are followed properly. Our Creator has given mankind a roadmap to success and has given us the freedom to follow it or not. He has sent previous prophets and messengers (peace and blessings be upon them all) to guide mankind, but Man has mishandled, rejected, and changed the previous revelations of the Torah, revealed to Prophet Musa (Moses) (peace be upon him), and the Injeel (Gospel) which was revealed to Messiah Isa (Jesus the Son of Mary) (peace be upon him).

Unlike the blatant and continuous changes that have been made to the Bible throughout history, our Creator has promised to preserve the

Qur'an, which is His final revelation to mankind revealed to His Final Messenger, until the Day of Judgment. Allah says in the Qur'an:

"Surely, We have revealed the 'Dhikr' (Qur'an), and surely, We will preserve it."

Surah Al-Hijr 15: 9

"No falsehood will come to it in the present or in the future. [It is a revelation from One who is Wise and Praiseworthy."

Surah Fussilat 41: 42

Although it is an obligation for every Muslim to share and convey the beauty of Islam to others to the best of our abilities, forced coercion is not permitted on any level. That mandate is clearly stated within the Qur'an which says:

"Let there be no coercion in religion. Truth stands out clear from error. Whoever rejects evil and believes in Allah has grasped the most trustworthy grip that never breaks. And Allah hears and knows all things."

Surah Al-Baqarah 2: 256

This verse of the Qur'an clearly states that attempting to force others to accept Islam is utterly impossible by saying, "Truth has been made clear from error," which indicates "freedom of choice" and the fact that, unless someone is voluntarily accepting to believe in and obey God, forcing someone to do so is unachievable. If one's heart is not into accepting something, someone, or a belief, despite clear evidences that justify doing so, attempting to force that individual to do so is futile. Equate that to the impossible feat of forcing everyone on earth to believe that Superman is real. Who in his or her right mind is going to plot and plan to achieve such an absurd task?

Additionally, gauging another's sincerity or intentions is equally

115

impossible despite one's "profession of faith" or actions, which give the appearance of one who believes. But those people may simply be "going through the motions", as the adage says. A person could tell you that he or she loves you with his or her tongue, but that doesn't mean that it is true in his or her heart. That person or group giving in to your demands to love you may have an ulterior motive looking to simply pacify you through deception, which should be expected if it was you that forced the individual(s) to utter such words in the first place. So how could any individual or group benefit by such a ridiculous campaign to coerce others into accepting something by intimidation, deception, or force? Logic dictates that such an agenda would be a fruitless and lost cause that no one in his or her right mind would attempt to undertake.

Most people are either going to accept or reject, while some fall somewhere in the middle –accepting half-heartedly, which equates to being forced to do something even if it is, they that are forcing themselves to go through the motions. Does it make sense to have someone who reluctantly accepts something that you cherish whole heartedly be a part of your family, team, or group? Would that be healthy for you or the group or team as a whole? Absolutely not! Therefore, clear paths and/or choices demonstrate multiple possibilities with a multitude of outcomes. One can do this or do that, go up or down, turn right or left but it is impossible to do any of those opposites simultaneously without being split into two! You would be dividing yourself, and logic dictates that that can't be healthy. The same applies to Islam. It is not healthy for someone to be a part of something that they have no genuine passion for. That type of individual would be placing everyone else in jeopardy because of his or her potential influence on one or more other individuals that could in turn jeopardize the sincerity of another and another and so forth, which only weakens the foundation of what you are trying to build.

Now ask yourself, if it makes sense to believe that Muslims are trying to, desire to, or even think for an instant that we would have any miniscule possibility of forcing someone to accept Islamby forced coercion? Common sense dictates that it is better to remove the weak links in a chain than jeopardize its effectiveness by allowing the weak link to remain. So be it with so-called ex-Muslims. I am not suggesting that Muslims should not be concerned about those that leave Islam (if in fact they were ever truly Muslims, Allah knows best) because as Muslims we should try to reason with them and try to examine the issues that drove them to their decision. It could be simply a lack of understanding or a need for clarification and proper guidance. Another issue that should be strongly considered regarding those that leave or reject Islam is that it is far easier to live life haphazardly in self-indulgence through personal whims and fancies, not answering to anyone, than it is to live a comprehensive and disciplined life of obedience to a being that you have never seen nor can prove exists.

Allah says in the Qur'an:

"We will show them Our signs in the horizons and within themselves until it becomes clear to them that it is the truth. But is it not sufficient concerning your Lord that He is, over all things, a Witness?"
Surah Fussilat 41: 53

"[Even] if you desire that they be guided, then verily, Allah does not guide those whom He allowed to stray, and they will have no helpers."
Surah An-Nahl 16: 37

Now let's consider why our Creator (blessed and exalted is He) would allow some people to stray. The reason is due to what I previously mentioned. Those people who are simply going through the motions are a detriment to the Mu'mineen. *Mu'mineen* is an Arabic/Islamic term, frequently referenced in the Qur'an, meaning "true believer". It denotes a person who has complete submission to the will of Allah and has faith firmly established in his or her heart; i.e., a "faithful Muslim". Anyone can claim to be a Muslim, but only

Kenny Bomer

Allah (blessed and exalted is He) knows if an individual is sincere in recognition and worship of Him. Allah (blessed and exalted is He) tells us in the Qur'an:

"It was We who created Man, and We know what dark suggestions his soul makes to him, for We are nearer to him than (his) jugular vein."
Surah Qaf 50: 16

As our Creator, Allah (blessed and exalted is He) knows the sincerity of the heart and He knows that some people are true believers and that others completely reject while another group accepts

Insincerely, and therefore those of the last two groups are left to wander in the darkness with no guidance or light.

God (blessed and exalted is He) says in the Qur'an:

"Their similitude is that of a man who kindled a fire. When it lighted all around him, Allah took away their light and left them in utter darkness, so they could not see. Unhearing, unspeaking, and unseeing, they will not return [to the path]."
Surah Al-Baqarah 2: 17-18

Even those who leave Islam are simply allowed to leave, which is contrary to the popular belief that Muslims will kill them. I am not suggesting that killing people for apostacy has never taken place. What I am trying to point out is the fact that this issue has been presented in the media as being one of the fundamental actions and beliefs in Islam, while the explanation for such actions have been left out or taken out of context routinely. People have been made to believe that a "blood-in; blood-out" rule exists in Islam, which forces people to accept Islam for life or die! Have you seen this happen? Have you or anyone that you know personally seen this take place? Of course, you have heard of this taking place in the media's onslaught against Islam, but do you have verified proof or eye witnesses to support such ridiculous claims?

118

No, you don't. So why believe something that is based on secondhand information without looking into the facts on your own? Do you trust everything that you hear without questioning it? Stop and consider the vast number of prominent people that have been caught up in scandals and corruption and the lies that have been propagated while attempting to achieve their agendas. Are we to assume that what we hear is legitimate and just accept it, or should we investigate any given topic through verified and legitimate sources?

The term *"FAKE NEWS"* is very common nowadays, but does that mean that the existence of fake news or false information being spread throughout the masses of society is a new concept? Consider the word *propaganda* as it is defined and how Adolph Hitler used it against Jewish people in Germany, leading people to believe Jewish people were sub-human. Compare that to the attacks against Muslims today. The attacks are very similar.

prop·a·gan·da: derogatory information, especially of a biased or misleading nature, used to promote or publicize a particular political cause or point of view.

Now apply that definition to the context of what the Qur'an says in the aforementioned verse, "Truth has been made clear from error," and you will see that there are two clearly distinguishable paths from which humanity may choose. One choice is right, and the other is wrong. The choice is yours. This is further exemplified in the Qur'an by the example of past peoples in relation to the prophets (peace be upon them) of Our Creator (blessed and exalted is He) as being the best of examples to mankind as compared to those who live life following their own evil self-inclinations and indulgences.

One path generates good things for the individual and society, while the other produces negative and detrimental effects on the individual and society as related to the potential impact and effects of the individual's actions and/or influence on others. Sometimes the effects are immediate and obvious, and sometimes we see a residual effect in the results of the decisions we make. Each person has a choice to either travel a path of truth and righteousness or a path of error and debauchery. So, what does all this mean? The choice is yours! Your decision will make you a member of one of the three groups that I have mentioned:

1) True Believers
2) Non-Believers
3) Half-Hearted Believers (Hypocrites)

You can open your mind to accepting the truth and beauty of Islam, or you can allow anti-Islam propaganda to influence and mold you into rejecting even the desire to simply hear what Islam truly is and what it teaches. Whatever you decide should be your decision and your decision alone, so, as you read on, I ask you to rid yourself of any former outside influences and/or preconceived notions that you may have about Islam, and I ask you to honestly ponder, think, and reflect on your current and past experiences which have generated whatever current beliefs you may have. I ask you to consider what, when, where, why, how, and from whom you have received information which has influenced your current beliefs as you Consider Islam.

11
They're All Going to Hell!

Every religion has its own beauty, and I mean no disrespect, offense, undermining, or belittling of any religion, including Christianity. I love my fellow believers no matter what religion. My intent is to express my experiences in a manner to which the reader can relate. This is my taking an honest and unbiased look into the questions that I once had regarding the inconsistencies and contradictions of Christianity, which caused me to "revert to Islam". They are questions which arise in the minds of many Christians, although many may never admit to having them because these questions are seldom discussed openly. Most people avoid these topics because in Christianity people are persuaded to rely on faith and not concern themselves with things about God that are unexplainable. Hence the old adage, "God works in mysterious ways." Yet Our Creator has given us the ability to think, ponder, and consider things logically. Therefore, we should not accept things simply because it is more comfortable to do so; but instead, we should gather the evidence and not limit ourselves to traditional beliefs without thoroughly considering the facts and sources of information that we all too often think of as truth. Whether people are willing to admit it or not, we are all sometimes guilty of giving in to peer-pressure from friends and family, those in authority, or people that we look up to as "role models". For most, it is easier to just try to fit in than it is to remove themselves from the crowd and stand out as individuals. Moving against the grain of popular belief takes courage, especially when your beliefs are in conflict with people that you love and respect.

It takes a strong-minded individual to stand up and risk losing people that he or she loves and cherishes. Doing so often means that you are opening yourself up to face abandonment, potential conflict, and harsh criticism from those that would rather belittle and label you than stop to consider your position logically. Let's be honest: some people actually become angry when your beliefs or opinions don't coincide with theirs. All one must do is listen and watch, in order to experience the ugliness that regurgitates from people on opposite sides of the aisle, regarding the topics of politics and religion. These two subjects have manufactured the massacre of billions of people throughout the history of man, due to wars, slavery, genocide, and acts of terrorism, simply because people adhere to varying beliefs and often times refuse to accept anything to the contrary. People will plot and plan, slander, backbite, conspire, scheme, and some are even willing to kill and die for their beliefs. Standing firm in the faith of your beliefs is honorable and commendable but not when it causes senseless division of the masses. People in the United States are quick to claim that this is a country o, freedom and justice for all, but then many of them turn around and ridicule, condemn, isolate, and oppress others who utilize freedom in a manner inconsistent with their beliefs. It seems that the United States is a country of hypocrites.

Most people seldom read their Bibles, and so they rely on the preacher to convey to them what the Scriptures say. Those who do read their Bibles routinely may or may not notice or take into account the obvious inconsistencies and contradictions that exist in the Bible and also in the Church's interpretation of the Bible (whether it is the Protestant Bible, Catholic Bible, or Orthodox Bible). But if you are truly a seeker of the truth, you should take an in depth look into, not only the Scriptures, but also the historical and theological facts about the Bible and the development of Christianity, so that you have a more complete understanding of the religion that you profess to follow. I encourage you to research and study for yourself so that you can make a more educated decision about what it is you do or do not accept as truth.

My parents separated when I was about ten or eleven years old.

After moving from Houston, TX, my younger brother and I were abandoned in Freeport, TX, and placed into foster care by Children's Protective Services. We spent our teenage years growing up at a facility by the name of the Brazoria County Youth Home. That experience was a tremendous blessing from Allah (blessed and exalted is He). I hate to think of what might have become of my life if I had not spent my teenage years in an environment that had a structure like the youth home provided.

It was during that period that I was exposed to Christianity, by the examples of some very special people that I grew to truly love and respect, and still do to this day, for being the God-fearing people that they are. They were employees, or what we called "house parents", and they were very devoted Christians. They still are to this day. They are people that Allah (blessed and exalted is He) placed in my life at a very critical time, and I am so very grateful to Him for using them to demonstrate to me what it takes to live a Godly life. These individuals had more of an impact on my life than they may realize, and I pray that Allah (blessed and exalted is He) blesses them in this world and in the hereafter for their commitment to not only me, but also every other child with whom they came in contact. They truly poured out their hearts and gave all that they had in order to help raise and instill virtue and character in us, and they used their strong Christian faith in order to do so. May Allah reward them for their relentless commitment and dedication. Ameen.

We never missed church. We attended a Pentecostal Assemblies of God church every Sunday morning and evening, as well as most Wednesday nights. We also attended Youth Night on Saturdays, at which time we would play volleyball and listen to a message from the youth pastor in between games. But what I recall most about those Saturday night volleyball games is the gathering of approximately twenty to thirty teenage males and females into a room to pray. We would sit against the walls with the lights off, while Christian music was playing on a radio. We were guided by the youth pastor who would say, "Let the spirit move you".

Although there were times during those Saturday night volleyball games when people would pray seriously and shed tears, it seemed to be more of an opportunity to make contact with the opposite sex than anything else, in my opinion. I don't mention this to undermine the efforts of the youth pastor, but to point out events that transpired during my Christian experience that led me to consider Islam.

Up until the age of about fifteen or sixteen, I had no prior knowledge of Islam whatsoever, and I don't recall having ever heard the word mentioned until one particular church service. The details of that service have been forever etched into my mind. I remember them as vividly as I do the births of my two sons. I thank Allah (blessed and exalted is He) for that because it was the experience of that day that triggered a new awakening in my consciousness. I believe it is a consciousness that we all naturally possess, if we are honest with ourselves. It is an instinct that tells us that God is One. It causes us to acknowledge a higher power whom we seek during times of hardship and calamity. It is a power that is above Man and any of his human attributes. It is a sense that tells us that we have a Creator and that He is unique and beyond our ability to truly comprehend who He is. But somehow and someway, we know He exists.

The church was a Pentecostal church where "speaking in tongues" was a common practice. If you have never experienced a church or denomination such as this, then it could be quite startling at times, for both those newly introduced to it, as well as those who are familiar with this particular version of Christian ideology. Preachers of these denominations are often referred to as "fire and brimstone preachers" due to their aggressive and unapologetic messages of judgment and condemnation in fire, against those that have not accepted Jesus (peace be upon him) as their "Personal Lord and Savior". These types of preachers seem to utilize fear and punishment as a means of persuasion, when addressing their congregations. They basically use scare tactics in order to convey their messages of redemption and are quick to condemn people to Hell, whom they see as being lost for not accepting their beliefs. Sometimes that even refers to Christians of other denominations, who have different beliefs and ideologies than that of their own. This attribute of passing judgment is common among most Christian denominations in my experience, despite their claims against it.

Even to this day, Christians of various denominations debate with one another regarding the, "Once saved always saved" ideology, the necessity for "baptism", as well as the ongoing debate of "Trinitarianism vs Unitarianism", along with numerous other issues. So, it shouldn't be surprising to anyone that those who call themselves "Christians" would voice their opinions about people of other religions, when they have been debating and arguing among themselves about their own religion for centuries!

Despite these differences, many have fought and died during efforts to spread and preserve Christianity, yet the differences still exist, which is a fact represented by the approximately thirty-three thousand Christian denominations present in the world today [**source:** *World Christian Encyclopedia* by Barrett, Kurian, Johnson (Oxford University Press, 2nd edition, 2001].

Studying this subject in depth would be a huge eye opener for anyone that believes any of the numerous versions of the Bible to be the literal Word of God or fully inspired by God. I say this based on the fact that there have been literally hundreds of thousands of interpolations in the form of deletions, additions, extractions, revisions, and rewordings of the texts, yet surprisingly, many Christians still claim that the Bible is the literal Word of God. This brings to my mind verses from the Qur'an which say:

"And there are among them [Jews and Christians] illiterates, who know not the Book, but [see therein] their own desires, and they do nothing but conjecture. Then woe to those who write the Book with their own hands, and then say, "This is from Allah," to traffic with it

125

for a miserable price! Woe to them for what their hands do write and for the gain they make thereby!"

Surah Al-Baqarah 2: 78-79

Biblical scholars --such as Professor Bart Denton Ehrman, who has written or edited thirty books, including five New York Times bestsellers: *How Jesus Became God, Misquoting Jesus, God 'Problem, Jesus Interrupted,* and *Forged*-- is one of many scholars who suggest that the changes to the manuscripts of the Bible are the workings of men who have intentionally changed the text in order to fit their agendas. Ehrman is the James A. Gray Distinguished Professor of Religious Studies at the University of North Carolina, Chapel Hill, and is a leading authority on the New Testament and the history of early Christianity.

The manipulations of the most ancient Biblical manuscripts have resulted in utter confusion, for many people who don't know what to believe, due to the numerous contradictions and inconsistencies found within them and Christianity itself. This dilemma is addressed in the Holy Qur'an which says:

"O you messengers! Enjoy [all] things good and pure, and work righteousness for I am well-acquainted with (all) that ye do. And verily this Brotherhood of yours is a single Brotherhood, and I am your Lord and Cherisher; therefore, fear Me [and no other]. But people have cut off their affair [of unity] among them into sects. Each party rejoices in that which is with itself. But leave them in their confused ignorance for a time."

Surah Al-Mumenoon 23: 51-54

These are verses to which I had not yet been exposed as of the Sunday night service that I have referenced, but logic was telling me that something was not right within Christianity. There were too many contradictions and an unapologetic dialogue that seemed to contain a

"We are holier than thou" message to it. To me it was, and still is, unjustifiable and pretentious arrogance that exists within the Christian mind state. It is an arrogant mentality held by some, not all, which Christians either fail to address or fail to realize that they emit, such as the case for the words spoken by the preacher on that Sunday night, that inevitably changed my life.

During that Sunday night service, the full-time pastor of the church was taking a break, so an associate pastor was filling in for him. I don't mean to belittle this man by any means, because I know that his heart was in the right place and his intentions were honorable. I am not trying to undermine or attack neither him nor the church. I am simply attempting to express the circumstances surrounding that day, as well as others that transpired overtime, which led me to question Christianity as a whole. It was a combination of those experiences which eventually caused me to consider Islam.

I had heard this man preach before on numerous occasions prior to that Sunday, because he would frequently fill in for the fulltime pastor. The delivery of his sermons was more aggressive and a bit louder than that of the regular pastor, but of course everyone has his own personality and method of delivery, so it was a pleasant change from time to time. It was certainly animated and entertaining to say the least.

As I sat in my seat during the service, I recall the preacher leaving the pulpit and then walking down the steps so that he could get closer to the congregation. I am not sure why he needed to get any closer, because he was using a microphone, so we could certainly hear him just fine from where he was on the stage. As a matter of fact, we would have had no issues hearing him even without the use of a microphone because he was yelling extremely loud.

With that night being approximately thirty years ago, I don't recall the topic of his sermon, but I have never forgotten three sentences that he yelled out at the top of his lungs that have echoed in my mind ever since. I remember the sweat glistening on his forehead and the handkerchief that he used to wipe it away clenched in one of his hands, while gripping the microphone extremely tight in the other. With veins bulging in his neck and a strained and reddened face, the preacher yelled out in an extremely loud voice words that I will never forget: *"JEWS ARE GOING TO HELL! MOSLIMS ARE GOING TO HELL! IF YOU DON'T ACCEPT THE LORD JESUS CHRIST AS YOUR PERSONAL LORD AND SAVIOUR, YOU ARE GOING TO HELL!"*

I was instantly perplexed by this! I remember frowning a bit and tilting my head to the side, while pondering over the shocking and bewildering statement that I had just heard. It seemed to be an extremely arrogant and dogmatic thing to say, in my opinion. Of course, I had heard similar comments such as this on prior occasions, but I had never heard someone condemn whole masses of people, and mentioning them by name, with such condemnation and boldness. It was if he had said, "IF YOU DON'T BELIEVE WHAT I BELIEVE, YOU ARE GOING TO HELL!" But didn't Jesus (peace be upon him) say?

"Do not judge lest you be judged. For in the way you judge, you will be judged; and by your standard of measure, it will be measured to you."

Matthew 7: 1-2 NASV 1977

I remember thinking to myself, "How does he know? He doesn't even know those people." I envisioned the Earth in my mind and a dividing line between East and West, as I visualized and considered all the Jews and Muslims on the other side of the globe that were placed there by our Creator. They had no say-so in the matter. They are people that were born to be Jews and Muslims, and they are exactly where Allah (blessed and exalted is He) intended for them to be. So, I questioned how this man could pass judgment on them as if God loved him and those that think like him more than the Jews and Muslims that he had just condemned to Hell? It's as if he was trying to do God's work for Him, by passing judgment on the masses. But the Bible says:

"There is one lawgiver, who is able to save and to destroy: who are you to judge another?"

James 4: 12 KJV

Not long after the church service mentioned above, after a separate church service, I, along with numerous other people from the church congregation, witnessed that same associate pastor grab his wife by her hair while dragging her from the rear of their car to the passenger side door, where he opened it shoving her inside of the vehicle in front of everyone. That occurred because he noticed a hickey on the neck of one of his sons which obviously caused him embarrassment and anger, so his wife was trying to calm him down. That caused him to turn his anger towards her. The interesting element to that is that his son and the step daughter of the full-time preacher were known to engage in a lot of physical contact during those Saturday night volleyball games in that darkened room in the church gym.

The full-time pastor, who's wife was the piano player for the church, was eventually caught up in his own scandal and removed from his position. A church member, who happened to be a technician for the telephone company, was working on the church phone lines one day and he needed to check the phone lines, so he tapped in from outside at the telephone pole. He heard the full-time pastor telling a woman how aroused he was and how he couldn't wait to see her again. During that conversation, they also discussed adulterous sexual relations that they had with one another in his office at the church on previous occasions. That former pastor is now a city council member here in Houston, Texas where I live. As on numerous occasions, I seen that man on the local news this very morning that I write this.

I don't mention this to expose him and I would never mention his name, because we all make mistakes and we have no business judging one another. I mention it because each time I see him or hear his name on the news, and often when I think of Christianity, I am reminded of those experiences in the church that were a vital part of my rejection of Christianity and acceptance of Islam. Of course, neither religion, Islam is more of a way of life than a religion, should be evaluated based on the actions of the followers or leaders. But there are fundamental differences between the two, with one being a complete and comprehensive guide for mankind in all aspects of our lives when followed properly, and that way is Islam.

There was always talk in the church about how much God loves us all, and how merciful He is, and how He knows us better than we know ourselves. So, I thought, "Didn't God know that He was making all of those people to be Jews and Muslims?", and "Did God condemn all of those people to Hell from their conception, while knowing full well that most would live and die as Jews or Muslims?"

People hear messages such as the one that the preacher gave, constantly in Christianity, and so they become prejudiced and opinionated, and they speak as if they know the fate of those that disagree with their beliefs, while lashing out and condemning them arrogantly. That type of thinking and attitude is in total contrast to Islam which does not allow any Muslim to presume to think that he/she knows the fate of another. It is difficult enough to gauge one's own status at times, so how can we gauge the status of another with Allah (blessed and exalted is He)?

We live in a society filled with prejudices despite how vigorously people try to ignore that fact by pretending that they don't exist. We claim that America is the greatest country on Earth because of our freedoms, but then hypocritically criticize those who utilize their rights when their beliefs are contrary to beliefs held by others. There are some who refuse to open themselves up even temporarily to hearing other views or beliefs. So, they cling to what is comfortable and adjoin themselves with other people or sources that coincide with their beliefs, while condemning others who believe differently.

The fact is, we are so continuously bombarded by inaccurate and biased information that people begin to believe things without seeking legitimate knowledge for themselves. That is because most people are so preoccupied with life that they simply don't have time to research for themselves, or simply do not care enough to take time to seek out the truth. Yet unfortunately, they base their opinions on nothing more than hearsay. For many, it is easier to rely on hearsay than it is to take time out of their busy and sometimes not-so-busy lives, in order to do study and research. But hearsay regarding any given subject is often easily accepted and misinterpreted as facts, when in reality it may be a watered-down version of the truth, or a version that has been grossly and purposely distorted. But if you are willing to open your mind and set aside preconceived notions, as well as the popular beliefs held by the masses, you may realize that things aren't always as they appear. That phrase is somewhat common, but its message is seldom considered by those who tend to rely on sources of information dispersed routinely upon the masses, that cause the majority to believe that whatever is presented to them is legitimate. Such is the case with Islam.

12
Christian Condemnation Continues

In 2011, I was injured in a motorcycle accident when a man ran a stop sign and pulled out in front of me. As a result, I spent a number of weeks in the hospital. After being released, a friend of mine hosted a fundraising event to help pay for the Life Flight and hospital expenses. This brother is a man with whom I went to Brazosport High School in Freeport, TX. We became very close due to mutual interests in music as well as having been teammates in football. He is a Pastor in a local church there in Freeport, TX. He and I have never debated one another about Christianity and Islam, because we know one another to such a degree that it is not necessary. We both understand and respect one another's character and beliefs, so it has never been an issue.

The fundraising event was held at another local church, and I was grateful for the contributions that were made by those in attendance, for it was surely a blessing from Allah (blessed and exalted is He). I was happy to see that one of the couples from the Brazoria County Youth Home was there, along with their daughter. Other than them, I only knew or recognized a few other people.

I was wearing a kufi (prayer cap) that night, which is of no surprise for those that know me, because they know that I am a Muslim. But there were others in attendance that were made aware of my being a Muslim, if they hadn't already figured it out. A man that I did not know went to the microphone and began talking about his conversion to Christianity from Islam, which occurred a great number of years before. He said, "I used to be Muslim; yeah I was once blind, but now I see." Mockingly he said, "I used to pray five times a day and used to follow Muhammad, but now I have Jesus." "Hallelujahs" and "Amens" were being shouted out here and there. Then he went on to say, "People who do not accept Jesus as their personal Lord and Savior are going to Hell." Then he looked over at me and said, "I'm sorry, brother, but I gotta speak the truth." A "Thank you Jesus," resounded from the congregation.

So, there I was on stage, only a few feet away from this man that just condemned me to Hell. He insulted me, but most of all, he insulted Islam. I can't say that I was surprised, but I instantly felt out of place while in the presence of those "Children of God". The awkwardness of the situation made me question if people would have even showed up had they known that I am Muslim. Although I was very thankful to my friend for organizing the event and thankful to Allah for the money given, to be honest it only generated $415.00, half of which was given by the couple from the youth home. Of course, I was thankful nonetheless, and I only mention the amount donated because it made me feel as though my being Muslim was a huge issue for some people in attendance. It certainly was an issue for the man that felt the need to address the subject by sending me to Hell. It's as if he was saying, "How dare this Muslim come in here asking us for money?" while those in the congregation backed him with the "Hallelujahs" and "Amens". The fact is, I didn't really need the money. I was there to show appreciation to my friend for organizing the event on my behalf. I never asked him to do it nor did I tell him that I was in a financial bind. He simply wanted to show his love for me. I was thankful to Allah, despite the amount given because any blessing received comes from Allah. It was all a test.

I must admit that I was angry at the time, and, although it was very hard to avoid, I did not mention the issue when I went to the podium to thank everyone for their contributions and prayers. But I did profess the Shahada which is, "I bear witness that there is no God other than Allah who is Our Creator, and I bear witness that Muhammad (peace be upon him) is His final servant and messenger". Although I was highly offended, my intent was not to offend as I made my profession of faith, but I certainly intended to let them know that I would not be swayed by any peer pressure or by the opinions of people that most likely know less about their own religion than I do. So, I stood my ground with patience and dignity.

The Qur'an says:

"Invite [all] to the way of your Lord with wisdom and beautiful preaching, and argue with them in ways that are best and most gracious, for your Lord knows best who have strayed from His Path and who receive guidance. And if you expose them, expose them no worse than they embarrassed you [in denigrating your religion], but if you show patience, that is indeed the best [course] for those who are patient. And do be patient, for your patience is but from Allah, nor grieve over them, and distress not yourself because of their plots. For Allah is with those who restrain themselves and those who do good."
Surah An-Nahl 16: 125-128

There are numerous other examples that I could discuss about this topic of Christian arrogance and supremacy, which leads followers to believe that they can somehow condemn others to Hell. All of those experiences have caused me to examine and study the history of Christianity and its origin, as well as the gross manipulation of the Bible, in depth. Therefore, the knowledge that I have obtained shields me from the ignorance of others. Christian scare tactics and opinions will never persuade me to accept a religion whose followers fail to consider the facts logically. These are facts that are hidden in plain sight throughout the maze of jumbled confusion of contradictions and inconsistencies in Christianity and its various versions of the Bible.

The fact is, the knowledge that most Christians possess is limited to what they are told on Sunday mornings by preachers who continue to say, *"JEWS ARE GOING TO HELL! MOSLEMS ARE GOING TO HELL! IF YOU DON'T ACCEPT THE LORD JESUS CHRIST AS YOUR PERSONAL LORD AND SAVIOR, YOU ARE GOING TO HELL!"*

It is obvious that even preachers themselves all too often fail to study the historical and theological facts of Christianity, but instead choose to latch on to Scriptures that represent their ideologies while steering clear of those that contradict them. Or it could be that they are aware of the numerous discrepancies but choose to avoid the issues altogether in what psychologists describe as "confirmation bias".

All one needs to do in order to realize this, is to familiarize yourself with the varying beliefs within denominations, and then focus on what Scriptures they will utilize in order to support their respective beliefs. By doing so, you will realize that Christianity is in a subtle but continuous debate within itself, which may cause one to question which version is best? Or, out of mere frustration, you may come to believe that none are worth the time and effort. Who has time to study what thirty-three thousand different distinct denominations in the world believe, while trying to decide which one most suits you? It is easier for people to be led by tradition, and so that is what most rely upon, as they usually choose the denominations followed by their parents, grandparents, and/or friends.

Obviously, there are some Christian preachers who are aware of the facts surrounding the variations in doctrines, yet they conveniently choose to ignore them. Then there are some who stick to the given Scriptures, who are ignorant about the historical and theological deviations. So, is it not to be assumed that their followers are following blindly? After all, not everyone is a preacher, and therefore most don't spend the vast majority of their time studying their own religion or the Bible, and so they rely on the preacher to guide them. If followers do study, it is usually done by memorizing or becoming familiar with Scriptures and stories during Bible study, which is in no way an in-depth analysis. Those people generally have little to know knowledge of the hundreds of thousands of interpolations that exist in the manuscripts of the Bible; therefore, factual knowledge is either limited or non-existent. Yet those very people that are limited in knowledge do not hesitate to pass judgment on other people, both knowingly and unknowingly. Some will voice their opinions and condemnations boldly, while there are others that don't realize that they are doing so.

Despite there being some Christians who are extremely judgmental, there are many who are not. Those who are not distinguish themselves from the others as being true believers. Allah makes mention of those Christians in the following verses of the Qur'an:

". . . and nearest among them in love to the believers will you find those who say, 'We are Christians,' because among these are men devoted to learning and men who have renounced the world, and they are not arrogant."

Surah Al-Maeda 5: 82

"Surely, those who believe, and those who are Jews, and the Christians, and the Sabians, and any others who believe in Allah and the Last Day and does good will have their reward from their Lord. And there will be no fear for them, nor shall they grieve."

Surah Al-Baqarah 2: 62

"Those who believe (in the Qur'an), those who follow the Jewish (Scriptures), and the Sabians, and the Christians, and any others who believe in Allah and the Last Day and work righteousness will have no fear, nor shall they grieve."

Surah Al-Maeda 5: 69

"O you who believe! Be helpers of Allah as Jesus the son of Mary said to the disciples, 'Who will be my helpers in (the work of) Allah?' The disciples said, 'We are Allah's helpers!' Then a portion of the Children of Israel believed, and a portion disbelieved. But We gave power to those who believed, against their enemies, and they became the ones that prevailed."

Surah As-Saff 61: 14

137

Kenny Bomer

The Qur'anic Warnings Regarding Christianity

The Qur'an also has several passages expressing concern for the Christian practice of worshiping Jesus Christ as God. It is the Christian doctrine of the Holy Trinity that most disturbs Muslims because it compromises the Oneness of God (blessed and exalted is He). To Muslims, the worship of any historical figure as God Himself is a sacrilege and heresy.

"If only they [i.e., Christians] had stood fast by the Law, the Gospel, and all the revelation that was sent to them from their Lord, they would have enjoyed happiness from every side. There is from among them a party on the right course, but many of them follow a course that is evil."

Surah Al-Ma'idah: 5:66

"Oh People of the Book! Commit no excesses in your religion, nor say of Allah anything but the truth. Christ Jesus, the son of Mary, was (no more than) a messenger of Allah, and His Word which He bestowed on Mary, and a spirit emanating from Him. So believe in Allah and His messengers. Do not say, 'Trinity.' Desist! It will be better for you, for Allah is One God, Glory be to Him! (Far exalted is He) above having a son. To Him belong all things in the heavens and on earth. And enough is Allah as a Disposer of affairs."

Surah An-Nisa 4: 171

"The Jews call Ezra [as "the Eternal Scribe"] a son of Allah, and the Christians call Christ the son of Allah. That is only a saying from their mouths. They only imitate what the unbelievers of old used to say. Allah's curse be on them! How they are deluded away from the truth! They take their priests and their saints to be their lords in derogation of Allah, and [they take as their Lord] Christ the son of Mary. Yet they were commanded to worship but One God: there is no god but Him.

138

Praise and glory to Him! (Far is He) from having the partners they associate (with Him)."

Qur'an 9: 30-31

In Islam, Muslims are never allowed to suggest having knowledge of the final outcome or destination of another person or group. It is only Allah that is capable of judging someone's heart. Note what Allah tells us in the following verses of the Qur'an:

"O you who have believed, let not a people ridicule [another] people; perhaps they may be better than them; nor let women ridicule [other] women; perhaps they may be better than them. And do not insult one another, and do not call each other by [offensive] names. Wretched is the name of disobedience after [one's] faith. And whoever does not repent is among those who are the wrongdoers."

Surah Al-Hujurat 49: 11

The Qur'an often confirms that only God (Our Creator) is "the Judge" who judges among His creatures. We read:

"The Jews say, 'The Christians have nothing [true] to stand on,' and the Christians say, 'The Jews have nothing to stand on,' although they [both] recite the Scripture. Thus, the polytheists speak the same as their words. But Allah will judge among them on the Day of Resurrection concerning that over which they used to differ."

Surah Al-Baqarah 2: 113

We also read:

"[Mention] when Allah said, 'O Jesus, indeed I will take you and raise you to Myself and purify you from those who disbelieve and make those who follow you [in submission to Allah alone] superior to those who disbelieve until the Day of Resurrection. Then to Me is your return,

139

Kenny Bomer

and I will judge between you concerning that in which you used to differ.'"

Surah Al `Imran 3: 55

The Qur'an also emphasizes that God is the One Who requites people for their deeds. So, He will reward whomever He chooses and punish whomever He chooses. For example, we read:

"A soul cannot die except by Allah's permission, at a determined time. To whoever desires a reward in this life, We shall give it to him. To whoever desires a reward in the hereafter, We shall give it to him. We will reward the grateful."

Surah Al `Imran 3: 145

In my personal experience, I have found Christians condemning others time and time again, while the vast majority prove themselves to be hypocrites and those who simply take the title of "Christians" while not following Christianity properly. In the same way that not all Muslims follow Islam properly. But there are far more "practicing" Muslims in the world than there are Christians. Most so-called Christians are simply Christian by name, which is reflected in the night clubs of the United States that are filled with so-called, "Christians" on any given night.

"Ye shall know them by their fruits. Do men gather grapes of thorns, or figs of thistles? Even so every good tree brings forth good fruit; but a corrupt tree brings forth evil fruit."

Matthew 7: 16 KJV

If you were to go into any mall, sporting event, or night club in the United States and asked random people what their religion is, nine out of ten would most likely say, "Christianity", while being those who routinely consume alcohol and pork. They are the people seen buying beer from the man walking up and down the steps of the stadium

140

shouting, "Beer Here! Get your ice-cold beer here!", or they are those dressed in revealing outfits while drunk and twerking in the club. This example may sound a bit harsh, but it is true.

My intent is not to point a hypocritical finger at Christians or to insinuate that there aren't Muslims who do these things as well, because there are. I am simply trying to point out that, based on tradition and demographics, most people in the United States are going to claim that they are members of one of the 33,000 denominations of Christianity that exist in the world, yet they don't adhere to the teachings of Jesus (peace be upon him), and in most cases seldom attend church. There are many who attend church every now and then or on holidays while claiming to be "followers of Christ", making themselves out to be part-time Christians. Many of those same people are the very ones condemning others who don't believe as they do. Belief and practice only work when joined together and acted upon consistently in people's lives. The problem comes when beliefs are more traditional than sincere and when practicing is reduced to more of a part-time effort than continuous routine. This is another major issue that has led me to truly appreciate Islam, which is a far more disciplined and obedient way of life.

"Prohibited to you are carrion, blood, the flesh of swine, and that which has been dedicated to other than Allah, and [those animals] killed by strangling or by a violent blow or by a head-long fall or by the goring of horns, and those from which a wild animal has eaten, except what you [are able to] slaughter [before its death], and those which are sacrificed on stone altars, and [prohibited is] that you seek decision through divining arrows. That is grave disobedience. This day those who disbelieve have despaired of [defeating] your religion; so, fear them not, but fear Me. This day I have perfected for you your religion and completed My favor upon you and have approved for you Islam as religion. [As for] whoever is forced by severe hunger with no inclination to sin, then indeed, Allah is Forgiving and Merciful.

Surah Al-Ma'idah 5: 3

141

13
The Oneness of God

The most important element to Islam is the prayer. We stop for prayer five times every day regardless of what is going on, be it work or play. It takes great effort to fight off the desires of the flesh and our own weak inclinations in order to go to prayer five times each day. But Islam creates discipline in the individual that I have never seen or experienced in Christianity. This is not to imply that there is no good in Christianity, but Christians simply do not practice their religion as sincerely and consistently as Muslims do in Islam. There is no comparison between stopping for prayer at least five times each and every day with going to church once or twice a week. Islam requires constant remembrance of our Creator in all our affairs. It requires recognition of the prohibitions that Allah has placed on mankind, and therefore the Muslim must live in obedience.

Muslims do not consume pork or intoxicants because they are forbidden in the Qur'an as well as the Bible. But Christians routinely consume both. Muslims do not worship anyone other than our Creator, whereas Christians pray to Jesus (peace be upon him) sometimes and other times the "Father", while forcing themselves to believe that the Father is the Son and that He is the Father at the same time. This is what psychologists describe as cognitive dissonance, which results when a person believes two conflicting or contradictory things at the same time. This belief held by Christians is contrary to the natural inclination that we were all born with that which says, God is One. It is a learned belief passed down through acquired knowledge that causes Christians to believe this illogical belief. Some (Catholics) even pray to Mary the mother of Jesus (peace and blessings upon them both), and some pray to people that the Church deemed as Saints, even

Kenny Bomer

though the Bible has Jesus (peace be upon him) saying:

"It is written: 'Worship the Lord your God and serve Him only.'"
Luke 4: 8 KJV

Because the most important belief in Islam is the Oneness of Allah, it is important to draw the readers' attention to our *dawah* (witnessing) efforts to have a complete and thorough understanding of all that such a belief implies. It is for this reason that I feel discussing the dangers of *shirk* (worship of other than Allah), with focus on minor shirk, is extremely important.

For a person to truly believe in the Oneness of Allah in having no partners or equals, one must be conscious of the pitfalls that ensnare many people who fail to realize that they may at times give power and credence to things, other people, and even themselves, that should only be reserved for our Creator alone. Discussing such a topic is a means to glorify Allah as being completely unique and alone worthy of praise and recognition above anything and everything else in existence. Therefore, it is my objective to draw attention to those things which people knowingly or unknowingly recognize as having some type of power of persuasion or influence over either themselves or their circumstances, and to express the dangers of attributing power to those things, which is a grave and unforgiveable sin in Islam.

In order to express the importance of avoiding shirk, it is necessary to start at the very beginning and foundation of the Muslim beliefs in order to give a full comprehensive explanation of what the Islamic position is, and how to avoid getting caught up in this vital mistake of major and minor shirk.

Everything begins with the *Shahada* (Muslim declaration of faith) in believing that Allah is the One and Only God, who is without partners or equals, and that Muhammad (peace be upon him) is the final servant and messenger of Allah. For one to truly believe this to be true, one must grasp the full context of such a statement, one must

144

believe it sincerely, and one must apply it in all aspects of his or her life. This means that one needs to be familiar with the essence of Allah, as well as His accompanying attributes, and then make effort to avoid associating any type of partners with Him.

The next step in the process is to understand what constitutes as being shirk. This occurs when one purposely associates partners with Allah in some form of worship, as in the example of Christians believing that Jesus (peace be upon him) the son of Mary is the son of Allah, or Allah in the flesh. Christians often pray in the name of Jesus (peace be upon him) or directly to him, as is the case with Catholics who pray to Mary (may Allah be pleased with her) as a mediator between themselves and Allah. Each of these acts falls under the definition of major shirk. People who fall into this fallacy are referred to as *Mushrikun*, as being those who practice shirk routinely. Allah says in the Qur'an:

"Verily, Allah does not forgive that partners are set up with Him [in worship], but He forgives everything else as He wills; and, whoever sets up partners with Allah in worship has indeed invented a tremendous sin."

Surah An-Nisa 4: 48

"And most of them do not believe in Allah without associating [(others as partners] with Him!"

Surah Yusuf 12 :106

Major shirk is easy to define because the acts are obvious. On the other hand, minor shirk is less obvious but still very prevalent among Muslims and non-Muslims alike. Unlike with major shirk, pointing out minor shirk requires a much more conscious effort, and thus, many people fall into engaging in it unknowingly. This type of shirk is forgivable as long as it is acknowledged and avoided. It is also forgivable in situations where someone has committed minor shirk unknowingly. Minor shirk is the act of beautifying one's actions in order to be recognized by other than Allah. It constitutes "showing off" or doing something to be recognized by others as if seeking their approval along with Allah.

During his final sermon, Prophet Muhammad (peace be upon him) made the following statement in the sermon delivered during the Hajj of the year 632 C.E., the ninth day of Dhul Hijjah, the 12th month of the lunar year, at Mt. Arafat:

"Beware of Satan, for the safety of your religion. He has lost all hope that he will ever be able to lead you astray in big things, so beware of following him in small things."

The above comment indicates that all Muslims will be misled by Satan in some form or fashion. This happens when one is simply going through the motions during acts of worship, thereby nullifying the act or deed being performed. An example of this is giving in charity. Charity should be given in secret so as not to draw attention to oneself from anyone other than Allah. The act of giving in charity should solely be done for the sake of Allah and one's standing on the Day of Judgment. This draws the believer's attention to purifying his or her intentions. Acknowledging this is extremely important for the believer. It makes one aware of the purpose and intent behind deeds and actions, because, if the intention of a person is to receive the worlds recognition for the acts, then the only benefit would be a worldly benefit with all other blessings being negated in the hereafter.

Prophet Muhammad (peace be upon him) described three types of people who will be fuel for the fire on the Day of Judgment: the rich man who gives while looking to be recognized by the people, the martyr who seeks to be a hero in the eyes of the people, and the scholar who shares his knowledge in order to be recognized as being knowledgeable. All of these are prophesied to be drug off on their faces and thrown into the fire on the Day of Judgment.

Other forms of minor shirk are committed when one swears by anything or anyone other than Allah. Some people will make comments like, "I swear on my mother's grave", or, "I cross my heart and hope to die." Prophet Muhammad (peace upon him) made the following comment regarding these actions:

"Do not swear by your fathers or mothers or the rivals [set up alongside Allah]."
        Reported by Abu Dawood in Kitaab ul-Aymaan wan-Nudhoosd

He (peace be upon him) said, "Do not say, 'By the Ka 'bah', rather say, 'By the Lord of the Ka 'bah'."
        Reported by an-Nasaaee in Kitaab ul-Aymaan wan-Nudhoor

He (peace be upon him) said, "Do not swear by anyone except Allah."
        Reported by Abu Dawood and an-Nasaaee

Another way in which minor shirk is committed is when using something or someone as a good luck charm. We as Muslims do not believe in luck. We believe that whatever transpires only does so by the *Qadr* of Allah. This means that things happen in the way that Allah decrees. This also means that things may not happen if not decreed by Allah. Either way, it is Allah's will alone that should be recognized and not some idol, medallion, talisman, coin, rabbit's foot, etc.

Prophet Muhammad (peace be upon him) also warned his companions about the dangers of "secret shirk". Mahmood ibn lubayd said, the Prophet (peace be upon him) came out and announced, The Prophet (may the peace and blessing of Allah be upon him) said:

"Shall I not tell you what I fear for you more than the false Messiah?" The companions (may Allah be pleased with them) said, "Indeed, O Messenger of Allah." He said, "Inconspicuous shirk, as when a person improves his rendering of the Salat (formal prayer) when he knows that others are watching."

147

The above hadith once again draws attention to the purity or lack thereof regarding one's intentions. It is something that all believers must avoid. Because shirk is the only unforgiveable sin, this topic should be on the minds and lips of Muslims consistently. We should remind one another of its dangers and by doing so, we as individuals are reminded to avoid falling into its traps. We should avoid giving ourselves credit during acts of kindness while being reminded that we can't accomplish anything in this life unless Allah first gives us the ability to do whatever it is that we attempt to achieve. We should also avoid going through the motions in our deeds for the sake of being seen by others. By continuously recognizing the mercy and greatness of Allah, and by praising Him in all things, we can avoid falling into the darkness of shirk.

The Prophet (peace be upon him) also provided protection against the inevitable acts of shirk by teaching certain specific prayers which may be said anytime. Abu Moosaa said:

"One day Allah's Messenger delivered a sermon saying, 'O people, fear shirk for it is more hidden than the creeping of an ant.' Those whom Allah wished asked, 'And how do we avoid it when it is more hidden than the creeping of an ant, O Messenger of Allah?' He replied, 'Say, O Allah, we seek refuge in You from knowingly committing shirk with You, and we ask Your forgiveness for what we do not know.'"

14

Rights of Women in Islam

PINK! It's a popular brand name strategically stitched across the backsides and the breast area of the females clothing apparel worn by females of all ages in today's society. Yet the connotation of the brand is overlooked and ignored because our society has been so bombarded by sexual innuendo and exploitation of the female gender that it has simply become an accepted part of society and culture in relation to self-expression and freedom.

In this brand's ads, we see sexual exploitation versus self-expression competing for what society sees as liberation for the Woman. One side feels that the female is truly free if she can dress as provocatively as she chooses, while the other side sees modesty and the choice to cover up as liberation from a society that attempts to dictate what is or is not accepted as beauty.

The rights of self-expression are promoted by sex marketers and pleasure seekers hiding behind the colorful screen of art, culture, and freedom which exploits the Woman and reduces her status to that of a sex object. We see this is in many professions such as modeling, dancing, the music industry, cheerleading, fashion, and the movie industry, which all fall under the genre of 'entertainment". Of course, women are members of other respected professions as well, but the ones that fall under "entertainment" set the standards for trends and fashions that are deemed as "in" as both men and women attempt to follow and emulate what is seen or heard via social media, film, music, and television, which casts a dark shadow over society.

This veil of darkness is a strategic and effective way of seducing women into subconsciously and systematically accepting a role of "sex object" while, at the same time, some in society are criticizing the

Kenny Bomer

veil or hijab worn by the Muslim Woman, and labeling those women of piety as being oppressed or subjugated, as if to say, a woman is only free if she demonstrates it by showing off her body in public displays of visual stimulation. But Islam is the light in the darkness of society that removes the veils of those blinded by misconceptions and misunderstanding. Surah An-Nisa (the Women), along with other verses of the Glorious Qur'an lay the foundation to uplift and maintain what should be a respected and honored status of the Woman throughout the entire world, despite cultural and geographic differences.

RIGHTS OF WOMEN

Islam heals and reconditions the hearts and minds of true believers and uplifts the status of the Woman to that of honor and respect. Unless one spends time in research and study, the inevitable result is that the individual will simply be brainwashed into accepting weak sources of information as legitimate. Sources that have grossly distorted the status of the Woman in Islam with rhetoric tainted with bigotry and misconceptions resulting in biased opinions about issues that most people have very limited true knowledge of. This is usually generated by individuals or organizations with a particular agenda for attacking Islam as demonstrated by the following quote by Leila Ahmed, a Harvard Divinity School scholar and writer on Islam and Islamic Feminism:

"Islamic civilization developed a construct of history that labeled the pre-Islamic period the Age of Ignorance and projected Islam as the sole source of all that was civilized – and used that construct so effectively in its rewriting of history that the peoples of Middle East lost all knowledge of the past civilizations of the region.

Obviously, that construct was ideologically serviceable, successfully concealing, among other things, the fact that in some cultures of the

150

Middle East women had been considerably better off before the rise of Islam than afterward" [*Women and Gender in Islam (1992), Leila Ahmed, 1992; p. 37*].

The attempt to undermine the beauty of the roles of women in Islam is constant, yet ironically in the Western world, women could not own property until the implementation of the Married Women's Property Act of 1848, which finally allowed married women to own and control property in their own right without the husbands' consent. But this right was afforded to women through Islamic rights of inheritance thirteen hundred years prior to that of the Western world, where in the United States women didn't have the right to vote until Congress passed the 19th Amendment on June 4, 1919, which was ratified on August 18, 1920, granting women the right to vote. This all was achieved under the Women's Rights Movement, which lasted from 1848–1920. While today in the United States women still fight the battle of "equal pay for equal work". Yet Islam was founded while Prophet Muhammad (peace be upon him) was married to his first wife Khadijah (may Allah be pleased with her) who was fifteen years older than he and his employer.

Although Khadijah (may Allah be pleased with her) was wealthy and independent, most women were not during the pre-Islamic Arab civilization. This civilization, before Islam, was labeled "The Age of Ignorance" *(Jahaliya)*. This was a time when female infanticide was common practice, and women were routinely seen dancing naked around the Kaaba. Women were treated like sex slaves and were inherited like property by debtors if the deceased owed someone financially at the time of his death.

It was Islam that uplifted the status of women, setting them free and establishing their rights while laying the foundation for how the Woman is to be treated and respected.

As the Qur'an says:

Kenny Bomer

"O mankind! Reverence your Guardian-Lord who created you from a single soul; created of like nature His mate, and from them twain scattered [like seeds] countless men and women. Reverence Allah through whom you demand your mutual (rights), and (reverence) the wombs [that bore you], for Allah ever watches over you."

Surah Al Nisa 4: 1

This verse demonstrates the equality of Man and Woman by addressing all of mankind irrespective of gender, race, or social status and drawing attention to rights to and from one another, while demanding respect for women as the bearers of child birth.

This reference of Adam and *Hawwa* (Eve) should additionally be considered due to their meanings. Adam meaning 'one created from a lifeless substance (clay)' and Hawwameaning 'one created from a living substance (rib of Adam)', which is a way of honoring the Woman. Hawwa was created as a mate and equal companion to Adam (peace and blessings be upon him) and this is further expounded upon in the Qur'an:

"The Creator of the heavens and the earth has made for you mates from yourselves and for the cattle [also] mates. By this means He creates you [in the wombs]. There is nothing like unto Him, and He is the All-Hearer, the All-Seer."

Surah Ash Shurah 42: 11

Islam does not share the Biblical view, which depicts and condemns the Woman as having been manipulated by Satan and seducing Man into partaking of the fruit:

"Unto the Woman he said, 'I will greatly multiply your sorrow and your conception; in sorrow you shalt bring forth children; and your desire shall for your husband, and he shall rule over you.'"

Genesis 3:16 KJV

This condemnation of Eve does not exist in the Qur'an where both she and Adam are depicted as equally guilty, yet only Adam was admonished. In Islam, pains and discomforts associated with child birth and the monthly menstrual cycles are a means of expiation of one's sins and elevation of one's status with Allah (blessed and exalted is He).

If she is patient and expecting reward from Allah, then, in addition to having sins removed, the woman will also be rewarded and have good deeds recorded for her. Islam does not reduce the woman to being ruled over by the husband, but instead says in a Hadith narrated by Abu Hurairah:

"Treat Women nicely, for a woman is created from a rib and the most curved portion of the rib is its upper portion, so, if you should try to straighten it, it will break, but if you leave it as it is, it will remain crooked. So, treat women nicely."

Bukhari: 3135

The Qur'an addresses the status of Man and Woman in many places noting the equality between them in the sight of Allah (blessed and exalted is He) with faith and obedience as the only distinguishing factor. One example:

"Whoever works righteousness --man or woman-- and has faith, verily to him will We give a new life, a life that is good and pure, and We will bestow on such their reward according to the best of their actions."

Surah An-Nahl 16: 97

Prophet Muhammed (peace upon him) said:

"Paradise is under the feet of the mother."

Mustadrak al-Wasāil, vol. 15, pg. 180

153

Surely if one were to consider and ponder on this verse and Hadith, one must come to the logical conclusion that the status of women in Islam is one of equality, honor, and respect. This is a status that is unique and elevated above that of men in certain aspects of life; it draws special attention to her attributes, which play a crucial part in the balance of humanity.

SPIRITUAL RIGHTS

Allah (SWT) makes it absolutely clear that He looks upon all of humankind equally:

"Indeed, for the Muslim men and Muslim women, the believing men and believing women, the obedient men and obedient women, the truthful men and truthful women, the patient men and patient women, the humble men and humble women, the charitable men and charitable women, the fasting men and fasting women, the men who guard their private parts and the women who do so, and the men who remember Allah often and the women who do so, Allah has prepared forgiveness and a great reward."

Surah Al-Azhab 33: 35

Gender, ethnicity, and social status do not come into account. One's status is only determined by faith and actions, in the obedience of Allah (blessed and exalted is He).

RIGHTS OF INHERITANCE

Rights of inheritance takes approximately six months of intensive study in order to fully grasp all of the dynamics involved, but the main topic is that the woman is free to keep all inheritance for herself. She is not obligated to spend her inheritance on the family as it is the man's responsibility to clothe, feed, and shelter the family.

"These are the limits (set by) Allah [or ordainments as regards laws of Inheritance], and whosoever obeys Allah and His Messenger [Muhammad] will be admitted to gardens under which rivers flow [in Paradise], to abide therein, and that will be the great success."

Surah An-Nisa 4: 13

MOTHER'S RIGHTS

In a Hadith narrated by Sahih Bukhari:

"Prophet Muhammad (peace be upon him) was asked, 'Who deserves maximum love and compassion in this world?" to which the Prophet (pbuh) replied, "Your Mother." He (pbuh) was asked this question two more times to which he again replied, "Your Mother." The fourth question was the same, and Prophet Muhammad (pbuh) then replied, "Your Father."

Book of Manners, Vol. 8, #5971

In this it is obvious that the Woman in Islam holds a special ranking above Man in some aspects.

SISTER'S RIGHTS

Regardless of relationship status, women are to be respected in accordance with the following verse of the Qur'an which addresses family and neighbor alike in regards to how women are to be treated.

"The believers, men and women, are Auliya' [helpers, supporters, friends, protectors] of one another."

Surah al-Taubah 9: 71

This means that all of humanity should be respected on equal grounds and that one should treat others with the same kindness allotted to one's own family. The fact that Allah (blessed and exalted is He) addresses believing men and women demonstrates that both genders are looked upon equally.

WIFE'S RIGHTS

The wife in Islam is considered as a fortress against the Devil, as derived from the definition of the word *Muhsina*, which means, "doer of good". This is referring to a pious woman who helps keep her husband on the straight path. The wife in Islam is to be treated as a gift as a way of thanking Allah (blessed and exalted is He) for her.

The following verse expresses not only equality but also elevation of Woman as a comfort to Man.

"And among His Signs is that He created for you wives from among yourselves that you may find repose in them, and He has put between you affection and mercy. Verily, in that are indeed signs for a people who reflect."

Surah Ar-Rum 30: 21

Unlike Western marriage customs, the woman has the option of keeping her maiden name, and the man is responsible for her financially in marriage irrespective of their individual financial statuses. Additionally, if the woman chooses to work, the pay she earns belongs to her alone as she is not obligated to spend it on the household. The same holds true for any inheritance that she might receive which is in contrast to the Bible's position on inheritance which totally excludes the wife from receiving any inheritance in Numbers 27: 8.

The Qur'an says:

"Men are in charge of women by [right of] what Allah has given one over the other [strength] and what they spend [for maintenance] from their wealth."

Surah An-Nisa 4: 34

This means that men have one degree of additional responsibility and service towards the woman due to physical attributes. Men are to protect and provide for the women which is a way of honoring them. The man is responsible for all financial burdens of the family and his wife. Before marriage, the father and brother are responsible for the woman, while after marriage, the responsibility falls on the husband and son.

The Qur'an admonishes those men who oppress or ill-treat women:

"O you who believe! You are forbidden to inherit women against their will. Nor should you treat them with harshness that you may take away part of the dowry you have given them, unless they have become guilty of open lewdness. On the contrary, live with them on a footing of kindness and equity. If you take a dislike to them, it may be that you dislike something, and Allah will bring about through it a great deal of good."

Surah An-Nisa 4: 19

Women are not rewards for men, and even some Muslims have trouble understanding a certain verse from the Qur'an:

If you worry that you will not be able to treat orphans fairly, marry from among the [widowed or orphaned] women as appropriate for you. You may marry two, three, or four. If you worry that you will not be able to treat them fairly, then marry only one [free woman] or one of the [war widows or orphans] that you rightfully possess [as prisoners of war]. This will prevent you from being unjust.

Surah An-Nisa 4: 3

Another verse says:

[If you have more than one wife,] you will not be able to be completely fair with your wives no matter how much you want (fairness). Do not pay too much attention to one wife and ignore

157

another. To do so would leave (the ignored wife) in the predicament of having but not having a husband. If you come to correct terms and revere Allah, then certainly Allah is Most Forgiving, Most Merciful.

Surah An-Nisa 4: 129

Surah 4: 3 does not give a man a "right" to four wives; instead, it gives him an obligation in certain, specific situations as a type of welfare system for single mothers and widows. In her rendering of the Qur'an, author Linda "iLham Barto writes a footnote to Surah 4: 3:

In view of Chapter 4: 129, scholars conclude that it is recommended that a man be married to only one woman, but there are conditions under which he may take the responsibility for up to four wives. Verse 3 is not meant to give men a source of pleasure at the expense of women. The verse should not be exploited as a way for a man to satisfy unrestrained lust. Having more than one wife is a great responsibility to be undertaken only under certain circumstances. An example is when there are more women than men, and the women are at risk from the standpoint of welfare. A man must consider the emotional impact that marrying additional women would have on the first wife. Prophet Muhammed (peace upon him) prohibited Ali (may Allah be pleased with him) from taking a second wife while the Prophet's daughter Fatimah (may Allah be pleased with her) was still alive. This was because the Prophet feared emotional harm to her if a second wife entered the family (Bukhari, #4932). Maintaining fairness among multiple wives is a responsibility for which the husband will be held accountable. Abu Huraira reported, "The messenger of Allah said, 'If a man has two wives, and he is not just between them, he will come on the Day of Resurrection with one of his sides collapsed'" (al Tirmidhi, #1141).

A Universal Message Inspired by the Holy Qur'an:
A Simple English Version for Young Readers and Youthful Minds
Rendered by Linda "iLham" Barto (a work in progress)

Consider the following example regarding a man treating his wives with equal fairness.

If a man were to marry at a young age while in poverty or while enduring difficulties which are common to young newlyweds, and then marry a second wife later in life when he was more financially stable and secure, it would not be fair to the first wife that spent a period of time struggling with him, while the second wife reaped the benefits of the struggle without experiencing the difficulties.

Now let us turn the tables. If a man married young as in the scenario above and he had children with his first wife, he would be obligated to at least attempt to have the same number of children with the second wife in order to give her equal treatment. This would be very difficult if the second wife is middle aged because conception in pregnancy is harder to achieve as women age. Additionally, the man would be faced with the financial obligation of providing for more people. This same obligation would apply for every wife and their children alike.

The myth of the 72 virgins is another stumbling block on the path of finding the truth of Islam. This is among several myths that have been embedded into the minds of many Non-Muslims while we as Muslims know this 72 virgins myth is a lie which is utilized to attack and make Islam a laughing stock. This myth may be rooted in what is considered and obscure and non-authentic Hadith:

"The smallest reward for the people of Paradise is an abode [for each man] where there are 80,000 servants and 72 wives, over which stands a dome decorated with pearls, aquamarine, and ruby, as wide as the distance from Al-Jabiyyah [a Damascus suburb] to Sana'a [Yemen]."

Sunan al-Tirmidhi Hadith, #2562

This hadith has a very weak *isnad* (chain of narrators) and is not considered authentic; however, it was reportedly included in a scholar's *tafsir* (explanations of the Qur'an) and picked up a following, and then it became distorted. A *Hadith* (teaching of the Prophet) must support the Qur'an, or it must be abandoned. There is absolutely nothing in the Qur'an that points to seventy-two virgins being on hold for suicide bombers. In fact, both suicide and killing (except in matters of justice) are condemned in the Qur'an. Consider the following three verses among others:

"And those who do not worship any other deity along with Allah, and do not unjustly kill anyliving thing which Allah has forbidden, nor commit adultery; and whoever does this will receive punishment. The punishment shall be increased for him on the Day of Resurrection, and he will remain in it forever, with humiliation."

Surah al-Furqan, Verses 68-69

"Whoever kills a human being except in lieu of killing or causing turmoil in the earth, so it shall be as if he had killed all mankind."
Surah al-Ma'idah, Verse 32

"And do not unjustly kill any life which Allah has made sacred; this is the command to you, so that you may have sense."
Surah al-An'aam, Verse 151

CASE CLOSED!

DAUGHTER'S RIGHTS
In response to pre-Islamic infanticide and the killing of female infants by burying them alive, Allah (blessed and exalted is He) revealed the following verses:

"And when the female [infant] buried alive [as the pagan Arabs used to do] shall be questioned, for what sin was she killed?"
Surah At-Takwir 81: 8-9

"And when the news of [the birth of a female is brought to one of them, his face becomes dark, and he is filled with inward grief! He hides himself from the people because of the evil of that whereof he has been informed. Shall he keep her with dishonor or bury her in the earth? Certainly, evil is their decision."

Surah An-Nahl 16: 58-59

Allah (SWT) prohibits the killing of all infants, mentioning the female in particular, and He rebukes and prohibits the mere thought of becoming saddened by the news of a female child.

Despite literal and figurative labels such as the brand name *PINK* as mentioned in the beginning of this chapter, or *oppressed* which is all too often used to describe Muslim women in today's society, women in Islam adorn the hijab and honor Allah (blessed and exalted is He), their husbands, sons, brothers, and themselves by concealing their physical adornments, and by doing so demand honor and respect for who they are mentally, emotionally, and spiritually. Those are the adornments that truly matter. If more people in society would take time to study and reflect on the high position granted to women in the Qur'an and authentic Hadith, and then attempted to live by the guidance that our Creator has revealed to us, divorce and domestic violence rates would drop immensely.

Women would not be marketed for their physical attributes, and young girls would not be "twerking" on YouTube, or taking photos looking back at their cameras in "selfies" so that their backsides are showing. Fornication and adultery would be less prevalent, and society would not have a backward view, which places more value in a woman's right to reveal than her right to conceal. Islam is the answer. Surah An-Nisa in particular administers strict and concise guidelines for those who believe and reflect. It establishes and directs humanity as a whole on the importance and status of women's rights –rights which should be solely based on the Qur'an and authentic Hadith, and not on the actions of people attempting to follow them.

Kenny Bomer

"O People, it is true that you have certain rights with regard to your women, but they also have rights over you. Remember that you have taken them as your wives only under a trust from Allah and with His permission. If they abide by your right, then to them belongs the right to be fed and clothed in kindness. Do treat your women well, and be kind to them for they are your partners and committed helpers. And it is your right that they do not make friends with anyone of whom you do not approve, as well as never to be unchaste."

Prophet Muhammad's Last Sermon: A Final Admonition

15
The Day of Judgment

There is a day coming of which no human being can escape. For those who believe in the unseen living their lives in obedient consciousness of Allah (SWT), that day will be a day of success. But for those who live their lives arrogantly, rejecting the signs and warnings of Allah (blessed and exalted is He), on that day they will surely taste the fruits of what they have sent forth. In the book *Christianity/Islam: Perspectives on Esoteric Ecumenism* (pg. 171-172), Author Frithjof Schuon summarizes a Hadith:

"Men who desire Paradise must not put their faith in the things of this world, that men who put their faith in things of this world will not have access to Paradise, and that men who put faith in God need not worry about either the Here-Below or the Hereafter".

Far too often, the human being goes through life seeking the pleasures of this world as if there is nothing beyond life on Earth. We often give ourselves far too much credit for our accomplishments and commonly seek the rewards that this life has to offer, totally oblivious to what seems to be the subconscious imaginary worlds of Paradise and Hell. This inability to truly understand the significance of this life in relation to the hereafter causes many people to go about their lives pushing the Day of Judgment to the back of their minds, as if this life is all that matters, living totally focused on the here and now. In the book, *A History of God* (pg. 262), Author Karen Armstrong says:

"God is not a reality that can be known objectively, but will be found in the image making faculty of each individual Muslim. When the

Qur'an or Hadith speak of Paradise, Hell or the throne of God, they are not referring to a reality that was in a separate location but to an inner world, hidden beneath the veils of sensible phenomena".

The significance of this is that if the human being focuses his or her attention on the Creator, the rewards for doing so will be manifested in this worldly life as well as the Hereafter. Failure to do so is of equal significance because by not submitting to the obedience of Allah (blessed and exalted is He), the consequences for that disobedience will also affect the disbelievers in this life as well as the Hereafter, but with results far more dreadful than the human imagination can comprehend.

Through the natural laws of cause and effect set in place by Allah (blessed and exalted is He), the human being has the ability to discern between what is right or wrong. This is a gift from Allah that we often take for granted. Allah (blessed and exalted is He) swears an oath in the Qur'an:

"By the soul and the proportion and order given to it And its enlightenment as to its wrong and right, Truly, he succeeds who purifies it, And he fails who corrupts it!"
Surah Ash-Shams 91: 7-10

Allah (blessed and exalted is He) has sworn an oath by His creation and Himself in this Surah calling man to ponder the importance of verses 9 and 10, which state clearly laws of cause and effect. For the one who is conscious of and turns to Allah in repentance and submission to His will, there is Paradise, but refusal to do so means that you will be fuel for the fire on the Day of Judgment. In the book *Eight Theories of Religion* (pg.7) by Daniel L. Pals, he describes Deism by saying, "It included the belief in a Creator God who made the world and then left it to its own natural laws, a parallel set of moral laws to guide the conduct of humanity, and the promise of an afterlife of rewards for good and punishments for evil." Various religions recognize this God-given ability of discernment that dictate the natural laws of cause and effect which produce the outcome of where we will spend eternity. In *Juz* (part) 30 of the Qur'an, Allah (blessed and exalted is He) describes the events of the Day of Judgment as a mercy from Himself so that mankind can reflect on this life as we prepare for that eternity.

The Great News

The majority of *Surahs* (chapters) in Juz 30 were revealed in Mecca and have a typical theme which causes mankind to reflect on the greatness of Allah (blessed and exalted is He) by mentioning the greatness of His creation and His greatness as our Creator. Juz 30 begins at Surah An-Naba with Allah asking:

"Concerning what are they disputing?"

Surah An-Naba 78: 1

People during the time of Prophet Muhammad (peace be upon him) as well as today have varying opinions about what will take place on the Day of Judgment, but Allah (blessed and exalted is He) has given us great detail about that day:

"Verily, they shall soon [come to] know! Verily, verily, they shall soon [come to] know!"

Surah An-Naba 78: 4-5

On that day when the first of two trumpets are sounded, every human being will die, and the angels will come rushing in to gather the souls of the believers and unbelievers alike. It will be as if they are swimming into the bodies of humans while removing their souls.

"By the (angels) who tear out [the souls of the wicked] with violence. By those who gently draw out the souls [of the blessed]."

Surah An-Nazi'at 79: 1-2

165

Kenny Bomer

All living things will die for a period of what scholars believe to be fifty thousand years; one day in the timing of Allah is like one thousand years for us. The earth will open up and spit out people from their graves and become empty, having asked permission from Allah to do so. The Earth will be stretched out to where there will only be enough room for each person to place their two feet. Mountains will be destroyed, and some will look as though they still exist, but they will only be a mirage. There will be tidal waves in the oceans, and some scholars believe they will possibly dry up. The sun will be brought close to people until it is only a mile away from us.

Uqbah ibn 'Aamir said:

"I heard the Messenger (peace be upon him) of Allah say, 'The sun will be brought near to the earth, and the people will sweat. For some people, the sweat will come up to their heels; for some, it will come halfway up their shins; for some, it will come up to their knees; for some, it will come up to their backsides; for some, it will come up to their hips; for some, it will come up to their shoulders; for some, it will come up to their necks; for some, it will come up to the middle of their mouths; and some of them will be completely covered with their sweat. Some will drown in their misdeeds. But those who are obedient will have the ease of praying two Rakat.'"

The sun will then, at some point, be folded up or extinguished, and the stars of the sky will be scattered and out of order.

"When the sun (with its spacious light) is folded up; (1) When the stars fall, losing their luster; (2) When the mountains vanish (like a mirage)."

Surah At-Takwir 81: 1-2

At the sounding of the second trumpet, every human being that has ever lived will be resurrected in body and soul and will come to stand

166

to face Allah (blessed and exalted is He) like droves of armies. Everyone will be naked in front of Allah but unconcerned because fear will be the only thing on our minds. Things that once were of great concern to us, such as our homes, family, and finances, will be totally absent from our minds due to the great horror and fear of that day. Allah (blessed and exalted is He) reveals this:

"When the she-camels, ten months with young, are left untended."
Surah At-Takwir 81: 4

People will be gathered in groups according to whom they followed while on Earth. The female infants that were buried alive, simply for being female, will be asked for what sin they were killed (Surah At-Takwir 81: 7-8). This will be to embarrass the people who have killed innocent people, such as the example of children killed by abortion today. People's eyes will be downcast and humbly subdued before Allah (blessed and exalted is He) in remembrance of all that He did for us and the effort that we made in return. Wild animals that are normally adversaries of one another will all gather in one place. Each person will be in so much fear that Allah (blessed and exalted is He) says that a man will run from his brother, his parents, and his own wife and children because he will only be concerned with his own well-being.

"That Day shall a man flee from his own brother. (34) And from his mother and his father. (35) And from his wife and his children. (36) Each one of them, that Day, will have enough concern (of his own) to make him indifferent to the others. (37) Some Faces that Day will be beaming. (38) Laughing, rejoicing. (39) And other faces that Day will be dust-stained; (40) Blackness will cover them: (41) Such will be the Rejecters of Allah, the Doers of Iniquity." (42)
Surah Abasa 80: 34-42

Kenny Bomer

Some faces will be lit up in happiness and joy, while others will wear frowns and be blackened because they were of the unbelievers, and they rejected His signs. Only the obedient people will be able to see Allah in His real form.

"Verily, from (the Light of) their Lord, that Day, will they be veiled."
Surah Al-Mutaffifin 83:15

Heaven and Hell will be visible to all people so that the people that enter Heaven will see Hell and be thankful to Allah (blessed and exalted is He) for saving them from that torment, while the people condemned to Hell will feel regret and fear. They will be told in a ridiculing tone:

"This is the (reality) which you rejected as false!"
Surah Al-Mutaffifin 83: 17

The angels of Allah (blessed and exalted is He) will be aligned in ranks, and no one will speak unless given permission by Allah (blessed and exalted is He), and when they do speak, only the truth will be told. The books of deeds for every human being will be spread out before us, and those books will determine where we will spend Eternity. Those given their book in their right hands will have an easy question asked of them. That person will have eternal success. But those given their books in their left hands or behind their backs will be grappled in questioning and will be punished and in eternal torment. They will beg for death as they enter Hell because they lived life not concerned with Allah (blessed and exalted is He) and sought self-gratification doing what they wanted.

Aisha (may Allah be pleased with her) said she once heard Prophet Muhammad (peace be upon him) say:

"By Him in whose hands is my soul, there are three occasions where

no one will remember anyone else. First, when the scales of justice are set up. Next when the books of deeds shall be delivered, and when the Bridge will be placed over the bottomless pit [of Hell], and everyone will be ordered to cross it."

Every human being that has ever lived will face Allah (blessed and exalted is He) on the Day of Judgment, king and beggar alike, and He will command the angels to weigh our deeds. Each person will be given their book of deeds, and each and every human being will have to cross a narrow bridge, which will be placed over Hell. The people of virtue will pass over it safely into Paradise, but the disobedient will fall or be violently ripped from the bridge by demons or thrown by their heads by angels. The bridge will be so narrow for some that they will lose limbs and be cut into as if walking on razor wire, as they fall into the fires of Hell.

One of the most significant events to take place on the Day of Judgment will be the questioning of Prophet Jesus (peace be upon him). Although not a part of Juz 30, this event is very important because it represents the greatness of Allah (blessed and exalted is He) and his dominion over all of His creations including the prophets (peace be upon them), and so in my opinion it must be mentioned.

"And Behold! Allah will say, Oh Jesus the son of Mary! Did you say to men, worship me and my mother as gods in derogation of Allah?' He will say, 'Glory to you! Never could I say what I had no right [to say]. Had I said such a thing, you would indeed have known it. You know what is in my heart, though I do not know what is in Yours. For You know in full all that is hidden.'"

Surah Al-Ma'idah 5: 116

Allah (blessed and exalted is He) will ask this question, already knowing the answer. His purpose for asking this question is so that Prophet Jesus (peace be upon Him) will bear witness in front of all of those who used to worship him as a god, that there is Only One worthy of worship. Jesus will go on to say:

"I never said anything to them except what You commanded me to say, which was, 'Worship Allah, my Lord and your Lord', and I was a witness over them while I dwelled among them. When You took me up, You were the Watcher over them, and You are a Witness to all things."
Surah Al-Ma'idah 5: 117

The Qur'an gives mankind an extremely detailed depiction of the Day of Judgment. If one were to ponder and consider the great vastness of the creation of the heavens and Earth and the descriptions of Paradise and Hell in each Surah within Juz 30, it should cause one to reflect deeply on the greatness of Allah (blessed and exalted is He). As we consider His greatness, we should realize the need for purification of self in order to find success on the Day of Judgment and understand its vital importance as Allah calls us to reflect on the examples of stubbornness and disobedience of ancient peoples. This is a true mercy from Allah because He has given us an awakening as well as the answer to ensure that we are saved from His wrath and punishment on that Great Day. That answer is Islam: submission to the will of Allah (blessed and exalted is He).

Completing this book is the most important and meaningful thing that I have ever accomplished at this point in my life. May Allah (blessed and exalted is He) be pleased with my effort, and may He be glorified and exalted forever and ever. Ameen

Various Quotes from Non-Muslims About Prophet Muhammad and Islam

Napoleon Bonaparte, quoted in *Christian Cherfils BONAPARTE ET ISLAM* **(PARIS, 1914)**
"I hope the time is not far off when I shall be able to unite all the wise and educated men of all the countries and establish a uniform regime based on the principles of Qur'an which alone are true and which alone can lead men to happiness."

M. K. Gandhi, *YOUNG INDIA* **(1924)**
"...I became more than ever convinced that it was not the sword that won a place for Islam in those days in the scheme of life. It was the rigid simplicity, the utter self-effacement of the prophet, the scrupulous regard for his pledges, his intense devotion to his friends and followers, his intrepidity, his fearlessness, his absolute trust in God and his own mission. These, and not the sword carried everything before them and surmounted every trouble."

Lamartine, *Histoire de la Turquie* **(Paris 1854), Vol II, pp. 276-77:**
"If greatness of purpose, smallness of means, and astounding results are the three criteria of human genius, who could dare to compare any great man in modern history with Muhammad? The most famous men created arms, laws and empires only. They founded, if anything at all, no more than material powers which often crumbled away before their eyes. This man moved not only armies, legislations, empires, peoples and dynasties, but millions of men in one-third of the then inhabited world; and more than that, he moved the altars, the gods, the religions, the ideas, the beliefs and souls... the forbearance in victory, his

ambition, which was entirely devoted to one idea and in no manner striving for an empire; his endless prayers, his mystic conversations with God, his death and his triumph after death; all these attest not to an imposture but to a firm conviction which gave him the power to restore a dogma. This dogma was twofold, the unit of God and the immateriality of God; the former telling what God is, the latter telling what God is not; the one overthrowing false gods with the sword, the other starting an idea with words.

"Philosopher, orator, apostle, legislator, warrior, conqueror of ideas, restorer of rational dogmas, of a cult without images; the founder of twenty terrestrial empires and of one spiritual empire, that is Muhammad. As regards all standards by which human greatness may be measured, we may well ask, is there any man greater than he?"

Rev. Bosworth Smith, *Mohammed and Mohammadanism* (London 1874), p. 92:
"He was Caesar and Pope in one; but he was Pope without Pope's pretensions, Caesar without the legions of Caesar: without a standing army, without a bodyguard, without a palace, without a fixed revenue; if ever any man had the right to say that he ruled by the right divine, it was Mohammed, for he had all the power without its instruments and without its supports."

Edward Gibbon and Simon Ocklay, *History of the Saracen Empire*, London (1870), p. 54:
"It is not the propagation but the permanency of his religion that deserves our wonder, the same pure and perfect impression which he engraved at Mecca and Medina is preserved, after the revolutions of twelve centuries by the Indian, the African and the Turkish proselytes of the Koran...The Mahometans have uniformly withstood the temptation of reducing the object of their faith and devotion to a level with the senses and imagination of man. 'I believe in One God and

Mahomet the Apostle of God', is the simple and invariable profession of Islam. The intellectual image of the Deity has never been degraded by any visible idol; the honors of the prophet have never transgressed the measure of human virtue, and his living precepts have restrained the gratitude of his disciples within the bounds of reason and religion."

Annie Besant, *The Life and Teachings of Muhammad* (Madras, 1932), p. 4:
"It is impossible for anyone who studies the life and character of the great Prophet of Arabia, who knows how he taught and how he lived, to feel anything but reverence for that mighty Prophet, one of the great messengers of the Supreme. And although in what I put to you I shall say many things which may be familiar to many, yet I myself feel whenever I re-read them, a new way of admiration, a new sense of reverence for that mighty Arabian teacher."

Montgomery Watt, *Mohammad at Mecca* (Oxford, 1953), p. 52:
"His readiness to undergo persecutions for his beliefs, the high moral character of the men who believed in him and looked up to him as leader, and the greatness of his ultimate achievement – all argue his fundamental integrity. To suppose Muhammad an impostor raises more problems than it solves. Moreover, none of the great figures of history is so poorly appreciated in the West as Muhammad."

Michael H. Hart, *The 100: A Ranking of the Most Influential Persons in History* (New York: Hart Publishing Company, Inc. 1978), p. 33:
"My choice of Muhammad to lead the list of the world's most influential persons may surprise some readers and may be questioned by others, but he was the only man in history who was supremely successful on both the religious and secular level."
Sarojini Naidu, the famous Indian poetess says – S. Naidu, Ideals of Islam, Speeches and Writings, Madaras, 1918

"It was the first religion that preached and practiced democracy; for, in the mosque, when the call for prayer is sounded and worshippers are gathered together, the democracy of Islam is embodied five times a day when the peasant and king kneel side by side and proclaim: 'God Alone is Great'... "

Thomas Caryle, *Heros and Heros Worship*
"How one man single-handedly, could weld warring tribes and Bedouins into a most powerful and civilized nation in less than two decades?"
"...The lies (Western slander) which well-meaning zeal has heaped round this man (Muhammed) are disgraceful to ourselves only...How one man single-handedly, could weld warring tribes and wandering Bedouins into a most powerful and civilized nation in less than two decades....A silent great soul, one of that who cannot but be earnest. He was to kindle the world; the world's Maker had ordered so."

Stanley Lane-Poole, *Table Talk of the Prophet*
"He was the most faithful protector of those he protected, the sweetest and most agreeable in conversation. Those who saw him were suddenly filled with reverence; those who came near him loved him; they who described him would say, "I have never seen his like either before or after." He was of great taciturnity, but when he spoke it was with emphasis and deliberation, and no one could forget what he said..."

George Bernard Shaw, *The Genuine Islam Vol. No. 8* (1936).
"I believe if a man like him were to assume the dictatorship of the modern world he would succeed in solving its problems in a way that would bring much needed peace and happiness.
I have studied him - the man and in my opinion is far from being an anti–Christ. He must be called the Savior of Humanity.
I have prophesied about the faith of Mohammad that it would be

acceptable the Europe of tomorrow as it is beginning to be acceptable to the Europe of today."

James A. Michener, "Islam: The Misunderstood Religion", *Reader's Digest* (American Edition) (May, 1955), pp. 68-70:
"Muhammad, the inspired man who founded Islam, was born about A.D. 570 into an Arabian tribe that worshipped idols. Orphaned at birth, he was always particularly solicitous of the poor and needy, the widow and the orphan, the slave and the downtrodden. At twenty he was already a successful businessman, and soon became director of camel caravans for a wealthy widow. When he reached twenty-five, his employer, recognizing his merit, proposed marriage. Even though she was fifteen years older, he married her, and as long as she lived, remained a devoted husband.

"Like almost every major prophet before him, Muhammad fought shy of serving as the transmitter of God's word, sensing his own inadequacy. But the angel commanded 'Read'. So far as we know, Muhammad was unable to read or write, but he began to dictate those inspired words which would soon revolutionize a large segment of the earth: "There is one God."

"In all things Muhammad was profoundly practical. When his beloved son Ibrahim died, an eclipse occurred, and rumors of God's personal condolence quickly arose. Whereupon Muhammad is said to have announced, 'An eclipse is a phenomenon of nature. It is foolish to attribute such things to the death or birth of a human-being.'
"At Muhammad's own death an attempt was made to deify him, but the man who was to become his administrative successor killed the hysteria with one of the noblest speeches in religious history: 'If there are any among you who worshipped Muhammad, he is dead. But if it is God you worshipped, He lives forever."

Kenny Bomer

Leo Tolstoy, Russian Author "War and Peace", "The Kingdom of God within You" (considered to be one of the greatest writers of all time)
"Muhammad has always been standing higher than the Christianity. He does not consider god as a human being and never makes himself equal to God. Muslims worship nothing except God and Muhammad is his Messenger. There is no any mystery and secret in it."

100 Life Instructions from the Qur'an

1. Do not be rude in speech (3:159)
2. Restrain Anger (3:134)
3. Be good to others (4:36)
4. Do not be arrogant (7:13)
5. Forgive others for their mistakes (7:199)
6. Speak to people mildly (20:44)
7. Lower your voice (31:19)
8. Do not ridicule others (49:11)
9. Be dutiful to parents (17:23)
10. Do not say a word of disrespect to parents (17:23)
11. Do not enter parents' private room without asking permission (24:58)
12. Write down the debt (2:282)
13. Do not follow anyone blindly (2:170)
14. Grant more time to repay if the debtor is in hard time (2:280)
15. Don't consume interest (2:275)
16. Do not engage in bribery (2:188)
17. Do not break the promise (2:177)
18. Keep the trust (2:283)
19. Do not mix the truth with falsehood (2:42)
20. Judge with justice between people (4:58)
21. Stand out firmly for justice (4:135)
22. Wealth of the dead should be distributed among his family members (4:7)
23. Women also have the right for inheritance (4:7)
24. Do not devour the property of orphans (4:10)
25. Protect orphans (2:220)
26. Do not consume one another's wealth unjustly (4:29)
27. Try for settlement between people (49:9)
28. Avoid suspicion (49:12)
29. Do not spy and backbite (2:283)
30. Do not spy and backbite (49:12)
31. Spend wealth in charity (57:7)
32. Encourage feeding poor (107:3)

33. Help those in need by finding them (2:273)
34. Do not spend money extravagantly (17:29)
35. Do not invalidate charity with reminders (2:264)
36. Honor guests (51:26)
37. Order righteousness to people only after practicing it yourself (2:44)
38. Do not commit abuse on the earth (2:60)
39. Do not prevent people from mosques (2:114)
40. Fight only with those who fight you (2:190)
41. Keep the etiquettes of war (2:191)
42. Do not turn back in battle (8:15)
43. No compulsion in religion (2:256)
44. Believe in all prophets (2:285)
45. Do not have sexual intercourse during menstrual period (2:222)
46. Breastfeed your children for two complete years (2:233)
47. Do not even approach unlawful sexual intercourse (17:32)
48. Choose rulers by their merit (2:247)
49. Do not burden a person beyond his scope (2:286)
50. Do not become divided (3:103)
51. Think deeply about the wonders and creation of this universe (3:191)
52. Men and Women have equal rewards for their deeds (3:195)
53. Do not marry those in your blood relation (4:23)
54. Family should be led by men (4:34)
55. Do not be miserly (4:37)
56. Do not keep envy (4:54)
57. Do not kill each other (4:92)
58. Do not be an advocate for deceit (4:105)
59. Do not cooperate in sin and aggression (5:2)
60. Cooperate in righteousness (5:2)
61. Having a majority is not criterion of truth (6:116)
62. Be just (5:8)
63. Punish for crimes in an exemplary way (5:38)
64. Strive against sinful and unlawful acts (5:63)
65. Dead animals, blood, the flesh of swine are prohibited (5:3)
66. Avoid intoxicants and alcohol (5:90)
67. Do not gamble (5:90)
68. Do not insult others' deities (6:108)

69. Don't reduce weight or measure to cheat people (6:152)
70. Eat and Drink, But Be Not Excessive (7:31)
71. Wear good cloths during prayer times (7:31)
72. Protect and help those who seek protection (9:6)
73. Keep Purity (9:108)
74. Never give up hope of Allah's Mercy (12:87)
75. Allah will forgive those who have done wrong out of ignorance (16:119)
76. Invitation to God should be with wisdom and good instruction (16:125)
77. No one will bear others' sins (17:15)
78. Do not kill your children for fear of poverty (17:31)
79. Do not pursue that of which you have no knowledge (17:36)
80. Keep aloof from what is vain (23:3)
81. Do not enter others' houses without seeking permission (24:27)
82. Allah will provide security for those who believe only in Allah (24:55)
83. Walk on earth in humility (25:63)
84. Do not neglect your portion of this world (28:77)
85. Invoke not any other god along with Allah (28:88)
86. Do not engage in homosexuality (29:29)
87. Enjoin right, forbid wrong (31:17)
88. Do not walk in insolence through the earth (31:18)
89. Women should not display their finery (33:33)
90. Allah forgives all sins (39:53)
91. Do not despair of the mercy of Allah (39:53)
92. Repel evil by good (41:34)
93. Decide on affairs by consultation (42:38)
94. Most noble of you is the most righteous (49:13)
95. No Monasticism in religion (57:27)
96. Those who have knowledge will be given a higher degree by Allah (58:11)
97. Treat non-Muslims in a kind and fair manner (60:8)
98. Save yourself from covetousness (64:16)
99. Seek forgiveness of Allah. He is Forgiving and Merciful (73:20)
100. Do not repel the petitioner/beggar (93:10)